IN PURSUIT

FROM THE STREETS OF SAN FRANCISCO TO WATERGATE

John W. Mindermann

JOHN W. MINDERMANN
and
BRIAN SOLON

AMES ALLEY PRESS

IN PURSUIT

FROM THE STREETS OF SAN FRANCISCO TO WATERGATE

John W. Mindermann and Brian Solon

First Edition

Cover art and design: Jordan Duvall
Front cover silhouette: Eisaku Tokuyama
Back cover Mindermann photo: Nancy Warner
Back cover Solon photo: Victoria Bassetti
Edited by Elly Rabben and CreateSpace

Opinions expressed are those of the authors and not the SFPD or FBI.

ISBN: 0615941486
ISBN 13: 978-0615941486

IN PURSUIT
FROM THE STREETS OF SAN FRANCISCO TO WATERGATE
John W. Mindermann and Brian Solon

INTRODUCTION

Imagine yourself in the center of chaos, engulfed in close encounters confronting menaces and threats—how would you react? Sometimes backup doesn't arrive in time, and you're that lone-star, frontier sheriff. The fate of the day hinges on thinking fast and acting faster.

As an FBI Special Agent on the C-2 Squad (covering "miscellaneous crimes") in Washington, DC, I was coincidentally tasked with weekend duty on June 17-18, 1972, during the Watergate break-in. My chance assignment led me to the upper reaches and inner corridors of power as fellow Agents and I navigated through deception and treachery, tracking the money trail, unraveling the conspiracy, shutting down the business offices of the White House, and precipitating the resignation of President Richard Nixon. Our scrappy team of C-2 Agents went head to head with the highest powers in the land, and prevailed.

Happenstance and a probing, inquisitive nature often put me in harm's way throughout an eclectic, almost rollickingly eventful, dangerous career. While this is my personal story, I didn't live it alone. These stories represent my perception of elements or circumstances, including realistic bits and pieces of the personalities of my diverse cast of co-workers, victims, heroic cooperating witnesses, and even suspects—my partners and fellow investigators might have different takes on what happened. In a swirling, ethically confusing subculture, with competing, aggressive, occasionally contradicting elements, we helped, guided, and saved one another, and I always strived to make the right call.

I'd been raised with cops—my Dad was a forty-year police veteran—and as I neared the end of college, I decided to pursue a career in the San Francisco Police Department. What awaited me was the daunting task of "maintaining the social order" in turbulent 1960's San Francisco—one of the world's most fascinating cities, a gold-rush town with a volatile culture awash with double-dealing, and corruption.

Patrolling the streets with the SFPD, I engaged in heat-of-the-moment combat encounters with thieves and thugs, nabbing crooks, and keeping the peace. With my fellow officers, we chased bad guys through intricate hilly terrain, became embroiled in policing sit-in demonstrations and full-scale riots, confronting threats and crime during a decade of massive social upheaval. As a member of the plainclothes "Operation S" (Saturation) Squad, I targeted the most hardened, felony prone hoodlums, whose rap sheets vividly revealed a criminal panorama.

After eight plus years of challenging and stimulating police work, I joined the FBI, which eventually led me to The Watergate. By the time Nixon resigned in August 1974, I'd transferred to the FBI Academy at Quantico, Virginia. Over the next seven years, I conducted research and instructed in the brand new Behavioral Science Unit, where Criminal Profiling was born and nurtured, collaborated on the development of innovative programs in Crisis Intervention and Hostage Negotiations, and created a university-accredited course on Police Stress, which I taught at the National Academy and to local police departments at FBI "Field Schools" both nationwide and abroad. Fate led me to return to my hometown as an FBI Supervisor in the San Francisco field office, where we battled organized crime, investigated bank robberies, and apprehended terrorists and fugitives.

Police and Federal law enforcement portrayals abound in TV and movies. While early radio shows such as Gangbusters and Dragnet exhibited flashes of realism, representations seldom capture the emotional aspects of street police work, or the lurking, almost shadowy intrigue and prevailing, constant danger and menace our FBI Watergate investigative team endured.

Ride shotgun in the front seat of the radio car pursuing every manner of crook late at night through the steep, majestic streets of San Francisco. Experience enthralling decisions made behind the scenes in the chess game strategies of FBI investigations. Reconnoiter a dark alley in a driving rainstorm, pistol drawn, hunting shotgun-wielding bank robbers on the loose. Lessons learned through these dynamic encounters, breakneck chases, and simmering political intrigue reveal insights into harnessing your mind and muscle to get to the heart of the matter.

Part One: The Watergate

(source: Library of Congress)

PRESIDENTIAL
NO
PARKING
MIDNIGHT
JANUARY 19
TO MIDNIGHT
JANUARY 20
1969
INAUGURATION

1

SHUTTING DOWN THE WHITE HOUSE

"Hey Min, do you think they'll shoot?" About a dozen of us were marching up Pennsylvania Avenue toward our target, the White House, a casual mass moving with directed purpose. It was a gorgeous, late-Friday afternoon, April 27, 1973, and everybody was scurrying, running for buses and driving their cars out of the District for the weekend. In the midst of it all, passersby couldn't imagine what was about to unfold for this quick-paced herd of men in matching suits.

We proceeded toward the Treasury Building, which shielded the White House on our side, not knowing whether the Secret Service would be pointing guns at us when we arrived at the West Wing. We had clear orders but no established ground rules. FBI Agents were sworn to protect the country from foreign and domestic threats to the rule of law. The White House was home turf of the Secret Service, sworn to protect the president and his inner circle. Two federal forces pitted against one another, both loyal, both armed. Would they see us as allies or enemies? Most importantly, would they shoot?

In prior armed criminal encounters, I'd pondered this question—
"Will they shoot?"—many times, but *they* hadn't ever been another enforcement agency in a scheduled confrontation. I felt deep concern and
harbored real doubts. I'd interacted with Secret Service Agents many
times and found them courteous and professional, but I didn't know
what their operational orders were in protecting the White House.
Were they mandated to shoot "unauthorized" intruders? Would the
Secret Service perceive us as a threat and react, or overreact? This had
no precedent. Control is a slippery knife's edge—anxious people under
pressure quickly become erratic.

My mind raced but didn't lose focus. As a street cop for eight and
a half years in San Francisco, I'd confronted menace, danger, and vice.
My experience in unpredictable, blink-quick street enforcement, FBI
special training, and high-risk specialties made me the ad hoc go-to
guy for our leaderless group about to face a possible worst-case scenar-
io—a shoot-out on the White House grounds with the presidential
guardians. There were no bosses to ask for guidance—we were on our
own, isolated and moving. Our orders were specific and clear—now
performance was crucial. As bewildering and unbelievable as it seemed,
a team of FBI Agents was about to face off against the Secret Service.
I had to keep my fellow Agents calm. Imponderables, fear, and doubt
cooked an unsettling stew. Speculation breeds overreaction. One must
project confidence to strengthen tempered resolve. Focus zeroes in on
controlled, successful execution.

"No, there's not going to be an armed stand-off or a shoot-out. Secret
Service Agents are professional and rational, just like us." Even as I said
these words, I wasn't certain. One panicked Secret Service Agent's er-
rant shot could trigger all the guns answering. President Nixon could
be in the White House. If he knew the FBI was en route to shut it
down, what might he order and would the Secret Service follow those

orders? We didn't know if any agreement had been reached between our boss and the Secret Service. Our impression was—it hadn't.

Twenty minutes earlier, we were summoned to a meeting by Jack McDermott, Special Agent in Charge (SAC) of the FBI's Washington Field Office (WFO). He'd replaced SAC Bob Kunkel, who was fair, formal, and reserved. McDermott, on the other hand, was a product of New York City—personable and outgoing, not afraid to exercise his leadership or display his opinions.

Just before 5:00 p.m. that Friday afternoon, we arrived at his large, square office, where he sat at his desk, radiating a command presence. We stood facing him in a U-formation, shuffling expectantly, somewhat uneasily, with our backs against the walls. He was about to make a phone call. It was apparent he wanted us to hear what was to occur, a typically McDermott method of inclusively briefing Agents. This gathering was to be indelibly imprinted on my mind. McDermott, who was always polite but quite direct, placed a call at about 5:08 p.m. to the US Secret Service. He was in fine form.

"Hello, this is Jack McDermott, Special Agent in Charge of the FBI's Washington Field Office. How are you? May I speak with the director of the Secret Service?" (pause) "He's not available? Well, give me the number-two man." (pause) "You say he's not available? Well is *anyone* there in charge? OK, may I speak with *him* please?" (pause) "Good afternoon. This is Jack McDermott, the SAC of the Washington Field Office of the FBI. Are you in charge of the Secret Service?" (pause) "OK. *On order of the Attorney General,* there will be about a dozen or so armed Special Agents of the FBI shortly entering the White House. They will be securing all business offices, including the president's—and they will not be allowing any files or any papers to leave those offices, or anyone to enter those business offices to take the files." (lengthy pause)

Apparently, the Secret Service boss-of-the-moment then told McDermott that the FBI Agents entering the White House would have to disarm prior to entry, causing McDermott to retort in a voice rising in volume, "FBI Agents are always armed! No, they won't be surrendering their guns to the Secret Service. I'm telling you that there are a dozen armed FBI Agents who are going up Pennsylvania Avenue to the White House. They're going to enter, and they're going to lock down and secure the business offices, including the president's. No paper will be allowed in or out. Good-bye."

McDermott slammed the receiver down and rotated his gaze, scanning the room to make direct eye contact with each one of us in turn, and asked, "Any questions, gentlemen?" We exchanged glances with each other and with McDermott. There were never any questions— the Bureau hired and trained us as Special Agents because we knew or could figure out the answer, regardless of the question.

"OK, just go up there and do what you're supposed to do. Enter and secure those files. Don't let anybody touch them. Don't let anybody in or out of any of those offices until you receive orders to the contrary." With such an abrupt ending, we had every reason to believe that there had not been an agreement between McDermott and the Secret Service regarding protocol for our White House entry and occupation. McDermott was very pointed on the phone, telling—actually, dictating—to the Secret Service exactly what was going to happen. This was bizarre, and we were stunned, absolutely shocked.

When we arrived at the West Wing and identified ourselves to the Secret Service, I'd never seen so many blue-lettered FBI credentials held prominently high, accompanied by the chant "FBI—Special Agents." The Secret Service indicated they weren't happy about our carrying guns inside. However, after brief negotiation, we entered armed and proceeded to lock down and secure all the business offices, standing sentry. There would be no shooting. Immediate potential disaster had been averted. Per orders, no paper was allowed in or out all weekend.

It was no small thing for the FBI to occupy the White House, and we as Agents didn't regard this as in any way ordinary. Americans have an inherent respect for the office of the presidency. But it was neither the Bureau's nor my way to place unquestioning faith in leaders, no matter their elevated status. We had a job to do in the face of extensive evidence of wrongdoing involving White House personnel. We were trained to be disciplined and goal oriented.

Meanwhile other high-stakes scenes were playing out. That same Friday afternoon, FBI Acting Director L. Patrick Gray resigned and Nixon escaped the DC political heat to spend the weekend at Camp David, where he told his closest confidants that he hoped he wouldn't wake up the next morning. He knew his administration was imploding. Attorney General (AG) Richard Kleindienst, in his memoir *Justice*, described Nixon's mental state the weekend of the FBI's White House invasion and occupation: "I don't think I have ever seen such a distraught-looking person in my life. The tired man, it seemed, bore the weight of the world on his shoulders. This poor beleaguered man began to sob—here was the leader of the free world, in an almost shattered condition. His sobs and distraught demeanor were profound and genuine."

Monday afternoon, President Nixon returned from Camp David, ill tempered and anxious. Approaching an office door, he encountered an FBI Agent, a young man with an accounting background whose physical demeanor did not radiate uncompromising authority. Nixon growled and shoved the Agent against the wall, screaming in his face, "What the hell is this?! These men—are not criminals!" Nixon continued to chew out the Agent, but the Agent, it turned out, had more steel than it appeared. He stood his ground professionally, not allowing the commander-in-chief to enter. Nixon stormed off in a huff, although to his (minimal) credit, he later returned, to the Agent's surprise and probable relief, and apologized for his prior behavior. The Agent handled this pressure-cooker situation coolly and valiantly.

Later that Monday evening, Attorney General Kleindienst resigned. At a White House cabinet meeting the next day, he recalled, "The President began pointing his finger at me in an agitated manner, [and] with an equally agitated tone of voice he was yelling at me about how terrible it was to station FBI Agents before the offices of fine, dedicated men as if they were common criminals." In a sense, he was right: they were decidedly "uncommon criminals." During this critical period of FBI occupancy of his seat of power, the supposed leader of the free world was gripped by wildly oscillating, desperation-fueled anger and depression, caught in a vicious downward spiral. Did AG Kleindienst actually call McDermott directly and deliver the order to shut down the White House? Kleindienst would deny it for the rest of his life, yet McDermott had been precise and expressly clear: *"On order of the Attorney General."*

The Watergate story unfolded in the pages of The Washington Post, chronicled by Bob Woodward and Carl Bernstein as a tragic debacle. From our perspective, at its core, Watergate was an FBI story. Our Washington Field Office C-2 Squad (covering "Miscellaneous Crimes") sorted through a minefield of political debris in midnight-dark moments to ferret out the truth. Watergate FBI Agents pressed forward, working relentlessly and collaboratively. Amid an unfolding scene of obfuscation, threat, intimidation, evidence destruction, misdirection, and meddling from an unpredictable, supersecret internal leaker, we had each other's backs.

Ten months earlier, when I received my first weekend call detailing the break-in, with its side notes of political dirty tricks, FBI/CIA perpetrators, and illegal bugs, I felt disturbing disbelief. As the weeks and months progressed, it seemed as though we were looking through a camera lens continually adjusting focus. Nixon's image was always in the background of the unfolding drama. Would he come into clear focus? Did this involve the president?

2

THE UNUSUAL SUSPECTS

(ten months earlier)

Entering the shower, I turned the faucet to begin the aquatic cascade. Seconds later, the phone rang. About once every eight months, an Agent of the FBI Washington Field Office (WFO) would be on call for weekend duty, and mine happened to land on June 17, 1972. Dripping wet, annoyed, and clutching a towel, I grabbed the receiver. "What is it?"

"Mr. Mindermann, this is the office."

"Could this wait a few minutes? I'm in the middle of a shower and will call you right back."

The male voice emphatically replied, "No."

Irritated, I grabbed a pad and pencil. He continued, "Mr. Ruhl, your supervisor, has asked me to tell you to pick up Mr. King [another Agent who lived nearby] and proceed to the Metropolitan Police Department (MPD) Headquarters and see the detective on duty. He'll brief you concerning a break-in at the Watergate facility, in which five men were apprehended within the Democratic National Committee Headquarters (DNC)."

I asked for the names of the arrested suspects and what was known about them. The clerk continued and gave me the burglar's names: Gonzalez, Martinez, Sturgis, Barker, and McCord. He hesitated for a moment before adding in a more concerned tone, "McCord is a former FBI Agent and an ex-CIA Agent." This break-in at the Watergate Complex sounded like a bit more than an ordinary burglary. Naked but for a towel, a foreboding chill swept over me.

Mike King and I arrived at the Detective Division of the District's MPD Headquarters northwest of Capitol Hill around 5:00 p.m. Recognizing us, a detective wearing a colorful sport jacket looked up and made eye contact. We knew each other from working together on a prior case, and he shouted to us from across the room. "Mindermann, ha ha, you've got this?"

"Yep." Seated behind their desks, the rest of the detective squad was tittering that Mike King and I had drawn the straw for this particular assignment. My eight and a half years as a street cop and four years in the FBI were overshadowed by veteran detectives of the MPD, with decades of experience involving crime-tinged political intrigue in our nation's capital. They knew this was a big one.

Smiling, the detective said, "Take a look at what I've got for you." With dramatic flourish he gloved up with latex protection and walked into a large, bank-vault-type safe whose door stood ajar. We waited expectantly as he strolled out like a circus ringmaster and produced a bevy of glassine envelopes containing brand new one hundred dollar bills, then fanned them out on a table. "Thirty-four one-hundred-dollar bills." Other detectives chortled as we noticed the bills' unmistakable newness and consecutive serial numbers.

"Where'd these come from?" I asked. The detective responded, "They were in the suspects' wallets, which they left in their hotel rooms at the Watergate Hotel." I'd worked a lot of cases, but none where the burglars had $3,400 in cash (nearly $20,000 in today's dollars). Thus began my baptism into the investigation of the infamous Watergate break-in. The detectives laid out the basics of how the men were apprehended: within the DNC Headquarters in the process of removing, or having on their persons, illegal or surreptitious electronic listening devices. Mere possession of these devices was a federal felony, over which the FBI had clear jurisdiction, referred to as "IOC" from the applicable statute—Interception of Communication. We did not have to prove purchase, interstate transportation, intent to use, or actual usage.

On the previous Friday, June 16, the night-duty clerk in WFO was in the midst of performing his varied and sundry duties—receiving telephone calls, notifications, and teletype messages; filing; and patrolling the premises—when at 8:30 p.m. he overheard the MPD radio dispatcher assign a marked patrol car a "run" to the Watergate on a possible burglary. Frank Willis, a security guard making his rounds, noted a single piece of duct tape affixed on the locking mechanism of a staircase door. He removed the tape, continued making his rounds, and returned ten minutes later to find another piece of tape similarly placed. What might be going on here? Willis called the cops.

After a few minutes, the voice of an officer assigned to the Watergate run came over the air reporting a "vehicle breakdown." Communications inquired, "What kind of breakdown?" There was a slight hesitancy, followed by a voice tinged with chagrin, answering, "We ran out of gas." No other marked police unit responded, possibly due to the heavy demand that Friday nights bring to the Foggy Bottom-Georgetown area,

with its nightclubs and restaurants. Other police in nonuniform attire and unmarked vehicles, variously dubbed "old clothes" or "scouter
squad" officers, were either filling out paper work or cruising nearby in
Georgetown along the Wisconsin and M Street Corridor. They heard
the exchange and told dispatch they would handle it.

"Burglary in progress" or "suspicious occurrence" assignments are
best handled by clearly marked units and uniformed officers. These calls
frequently result in searches in unfamiliar buildings and surroundings
where officers don't know the layout. Mix-ups and misidentifications
are always a risk, especially at night. Plainclothes officers are at height-
ened exposure of being potentially fired upon. Blending into the scene,
operating assorted non-police-appearing vehicles, and sporting their
undercover disguises, the plainclothes guys responded nonetheless. The
burglars' lookouts in the Howard Johnson's hotel across the street from
the Watergate Complex apparently failed to recognize them and gave
no warning to the burglars in the DNC HQ.

The arrested burglars were trained, hardened intelligence operatives—battle-experienced soldiers caught in an illegal, clandestine
operation with serious consequences and far-reaching implications
for our nation's most powerful political people. Three were Cuban
Americans operating from Miami's caldron of anti-Castro intrigue.
None of us knew how far their friends and supporters might be willing to go. Their overseer, E. Howard Hunt, ostensibly a consultant
to the White House, was in fact a career case manager for the CIA
who possessed an unknown array of skills and propensities. G. Gordon
Liddy, finance counsel at CREEP (Nixon's Committee to RE-Elect
the President) and also a former FBI Agent, was a firearms aficionado.
Bureau legend had it that one particular evening in Denver, Liddy
placed eight guns on a bed and asked his wife which firearm best
suited his evening's attire.

We approached our assigned duties with only a skeletal outline, no detailed briefing, and severely limited, almost compartmentalized, knowledge. Things were moving fast, and circumstances were fluid and chaotic. We foraged around a bit for alternative avenues of inquiry and hit upon a young attorney, Douglas Caddy. He identified himself repeatedly as being associated with the suspects (he was also ex-CIA, according to Bob Risch and Jim Hunt's book *Warrior: Frank Sturgis*). When we met with Caddy, he was circumspect, distant, and reserved, with a polite pushback, providing little information, except that he represented the Watergate burglary suspects, and our requests to interview them were denied. As far as we knew, we were the first FBI field responders sent from WFO to assess the situation. I later learned that assessments were conducted prior to the involvement of Mike King and me. Four decades later, I connected with Case Agent Angelo Lano, leader of the C-2 Squad's Watergate investigation, who sketched out events occurring prior to my arrival.

SA Angelo Lano had paid his dues. He completed law school in Baltimore, Maryland, while working as an FBI "Title III clerk" (responsible for overseeing the administration of the FBI's wiretaps) and supporting his growing, young family. "Ang," a Bureau veteran with substantial accomplishments, held high status and station within the WFO.

This particular weekend in mid-June 1972, Ang planned to accompany his boys to their important little league baseball practice. Awakened shortly after 6:00 a.m. by a phone call, he was told by the weekend supervisor that five men had been arrested by MPD at the Watergate complex, and the SAC wanted him to respond to the 2nd District Police Headquarters (where arrestees were being temporarily held), because he handled criminal matters in that area. He was to determine what exactly had taken place at the Watergate.

Lano emphatically stated, "The weekend Criminal Duty Agent [a.k.a. John Mindermann] should handle this request," and hung up. (Agent culture allows one to push the boundaries and engage in gentlemanly forceful dissent regardless of rank.) Lano was to quickly find out that this "request" was actually a directive. Two minutes later, SAC Kunkel personally called and ordered Lano to respond to the Watergate and to take another Agent along. Lano made his case to Kunkel about his "commitment to his sons' baseball practice," yet struck out, as Kunkel assuaged that he "wouldn't be out of pocket that long." Lano's "out of pocket" would turn out to be a super-intense, nineteen-hour marathon.

Lano was a logical choice to lead the investigation, as he routinely worked "Major Burglaries" (MB cases involved more than $50,000 in loss) in the Washington, DC area alongside the MPD Burglary Squad members. FBI working policy presumed that the loot from any MB would travel interstate; therefore we actively participated with local detectives at the inception of any MB investigation. Criminal Agents were frequently embedded with local police.

Police didn't know the reason or motive behind the Watergate break-in, and the five arrestees languished in 2nd District cells awaiting transport "downtown." True names or timely "identification" of these subjects was crucial, as such would bring to the forefront individual histories, backgrounds, associates, and possibly recent activities and commitments. This kind of information almost always provided the clues or guideposts upon which we could probe to develop pathways to the truth.

Lano and C-2 Squad member Pete Paul arrived at MPD 2nd District HQ and met with a Deputy Police Chief, Assistant United States Attorney (AUSA) Charles "Chuck" Work, and Sgt. Paul Leper of the Burglary Unit at the MPD. Work and Leper described the arrest of five men caught in the act of burglarizing the DNC HQ in possession of break-in tools, cameras, walkie-talkies, rubber gloves, and a gadget that the police initially believed to be "electronics for a bomb"—upon closer inspection, it appeared to be a smoke detector device, housing various wires, a nine-volt battery, and a small microphone.

Lano and Paul proceeded to the jail cell to see the five arrestees, who'd previously provided fictitious names to police. Each one refused to identify himself or speak with them. Lano and Paul then examined items seized in the arrest: two burglars carried room keys from the Watergate Hotel, located within the Watergate Complex, prompting AUSA Charles Work and a Detective to craft an affidavit for a search warrant. A duffel bag contained roughly fifty rolls of 35 mm film, two Minolta cameras, and—buried at the bottom of the bag, wrapped in toilet paper—a small, black, rectangular device with battery clips and wires designed to monitor telephone calls. "Electronic eavesdropping equipment" fell under FBI jurisdiction courtesy US Code Title 18: *Federal Violation of Interception of Communication.*

Lano advised bringing the burglars' equipment to WFO for review, and then tracing the arrestees' fingerprints to determine their true identities and see if they had any prior arrests. Paul made a beeline into the WFO where the Duty Supervisor preliminarily confirmed that the confiscated devices were indeed electronic eavesdropping equip- ment, and that within the District, there existed no known "manufac- turing system" for them. Agent Daniel C. Mahan (a.k.a. "Handsome Dan") responded to Lano's call to conduct a more detailed examination of the devices, as Mahan had expertise in this area. Paul rushed the fingerprint cards to the Identification Division, where the immediate processing revealed that the arrestees used fake names—"Ed Martin" was in fact James W. McCord, previously employed by the FBI and CIA. Circa 11:00 a.m., attorney Douglas Caddy arrived at MPD, saying he represented the five men. When asked how he came to represent them—since none of the arrestees had used a telephone—Caddy replied he'd been "contacted by another individual," whom he refused to identify.

As noon approached, Agent Angelo Lano arrived at the Watergate Hotel with a fellow Agent and a Detective. On scene, veteran *Washington Post* police reporter Al Lewis hovered in the vicinity—somehow he was *always* at crime scenes. The Agents and Detective searched the two rooms connected to the burglary. The first contained clothing and not much else. They entered Room 243 and saw that it appeared to have been deserted in a hurry—the sliding glass door to a balcony was left wide open, curtains blowing in the breeze, dresser light lit. On the bed: wallets containing sequential hundred-dollar bills, a small personal address book—property of "Bernard Barker"—and a metal, flip-up telephone-listening device—property of "Martinez." An Agent searching beneath the shelf paper lining of a dresser drawer discovered a stamped envelope addressed to a country club, with return name and address of E. Howard Hunt. Hunt's identity was known to the FBI because he'd previously applied for a position as a consultant at the White House, prompting the FBI to conduct a Special Inquiry (SPI) background investigation on him.

Agent John Ruhl, C-2's Supervisor, had previously overseen the WFO's applications division, a.k.a. "Happy Apps"; thus he possessed in-depth knowledge about SPI investigations. Ruhl quickly produced Hunt's background file and reached out to key people he knew in the District to provide supplemental information and determine Hunt's current "status." Noticing Hunt lived close by in Potomac, Maryland, Pete Paul and another Agent headed out to pay him a visit. Shortly thereafter, Agent Paul radioed in, saying Hunt admitted the envelope and enclosed check were his; however, he would not speak any further until he consulted with an attorney. A phone call to the White House revealed Hunt was formerly a consultant, working directly under Charles Colson (Special Counsel to President Nixon), and was reportedly released from his assignment in March 1972, three months prior.

Back at the WFO office, Agent Lano evaluated, consolidated, and refocused. He began working the phones furiously, with efforts targeting White House duty people, for information concerning possible connections between the Watergate burglars and presidential staff. Lano told the FBI Miami office that this emerging "Watergate" was "an expedite matter," and to institute investigations concerning the four Miami-based Watergate burglars. Lano requested the FBI Baltimore office to begin working on the background of the fifth burglar, James McCord, who resided in Maryland. Not missing a point, Lano contacted the FBI Alexandria office to begin inquires with the CIA at their Langley, Virginia, headquarters, to determine what role, if any, the arrestees had with that agency. While other Agents continued to work the phones, the duty clerk informed Lano that Henry Peterson, Assistant Attorney General, telephoned requesting information. Ang took the call, providing Peterson everything the FBI knew up to that moment.

Lano capitalized on his extensive working contacts generated by his background in high-profile cases. Between 1969 and 1972, a series of bombings along Embassy Row resulted in joint investigations by the FBI C-2 Squad, MPD Burglary Squad, and the Secret Service. Lano called his contact, Secret Service SA John Love, at home. Love had special expertise in tracing money, and he agreed to assist in running down the origin and distribution trail of the seized hundred-dollar bills.

Agents continued into the night, receiving updated information from Miami and Baltimore. The FBI Alexandria Office responded, indicating that no information would be forthcoming from the CIA until Monday. Love of the Secret Service also indicated the sequential hundred-dollar bills status would be resolved Monday. Around midnight, Lano authored a "summarizing teletype" for FBI HQ, then decided to call Kunkel—whose stern "directive" early that morning set the day in motion—because after all, Lano thought he "owed him one."

Saturday, June 17, 1972, was a chaotic whirlwind of assessment, controlled staging, educated guesswork, timely responses, and orchestration. Agents, police detectives, and federal prosecutors rose to the occasion and worked multiple scenes seamlessly, with Lano waving the baton, directing pace and inflection. The Bureau sunk its teeth in deeply, right to the bone.

Lano recalled, "Monday morning [June 19th], all hell broke loose," as a flood of data came rolling in. An Agent discovered that the sequential hundred-dollar bills were shipped from Washington, DC, to the Federal Reserve in Atlanta and subsequently put into circulation by the Federal Reserve Bank in Miami, Florida. A Miami Case Agent traced the hundred-dollar bills to the Republic National Bank, where Watergate burglar Bernard Barker maintained an account. An MPD Officer recognized a photo in *The Washington Post* of James McCord—one of the arrested men—and told the FBI that McCord was Chief of Security for the Committee to RE-Elect the President (CREEP). McCord had rented two different rooms at the Howard Johnson's, located across the street from the Watergate Complex, according to the hotel's Assistant Manager. Telephone records from McCord's rental rooms revealed numerous calls to New Haven, Connecticut, and to one Alfred Baldwin, a former FBI Agent who'd left the Bureau several years prior.

The FBI investigative locomotive was accelerating to express-train status, quickly becoming a virtual moving front and clearly showing the makings of a major incident, but who could conceive where the track might wind? Our C-2 Squad tapped into an aggressive mentality and mode of operation. Within days, a core conspiracy began emerging, with all signs pointing to CREEP as the entity behind Watergate. Under extreme internal pressure, CREEP employees were understandably evasive and hesitant, as their superiors forbade cooperating with the FBI, and coming forward could mean losing their jobs. Although CREEP employees were shielded by their attorneys, we were determined to obliterate any roadblocks, firewalls, and impediments deliberately placed in our path.

We were shocked and bewildered when critical information from our interviews began leaking to the press. The WFO held secret information tightly and securely, and we were sure there were no leakers in the C-2 Squad. It didn't make any sense because we knew the FBI—or believed we did. That apparently wasn't the case at FBI Headquarters. Angelo Lano's post-Watergate review of Headquarters files eventually hit pay dirt. Clear indications revealed that "several Bureau Officials" were also "leakers." At the same time, fingers were pointed at WFO's C-2 Squad Field Agents as "logical suspects" in this activity.

Years later, an angry, disillusioned Lano shared his feelings of betrayal over Bureau officials conspiring to leak information from ongoing C-2 Watergate criminal investigative efforts—but to what end or objectives? Undoubtedly Acting Director L. Patrick Gray was a target: he wasn't "Bureau" and his appointment was seen as a slap in the face to highly placed men, and detrimental to their continued ascendancies. As Watergate unfolded, these officials likely had multiple and continuing conversations about how leaks, or ongoing, "strategic public disclosure" would serve their agendas. Possibly their goals were to undermine or derail Gray's congressional confirmation process and simultaneously bolster congressional and public support for the FBI to get to the bottom of the mess. Their "betrayal," fingering C-2 Agents, may have been evaluated as temporary, collateral damage—just part of being a Field Agent.

Lano's continued efforts of surfacing and examining FBI Headquarters memos led him to observe, "Examination of the Bureau's 'in-office' or 'in-house files' tell stories and reveal interesting points. I recently discovered a time log and memo from a former Agent who claimed he received telephone calls from John Ehrlichman the night of the burglary. Ehrlichman ordered him to 'Shut down the case...NOW!'" Lano spoke with this former Supervisor on several occasions, and he insisted his notations and writings "are true facts." Why has this critical, revealing incident remained hidden? The receiver of the Ehrlichman calls stated he "wrote a memo"; however, no one apparently "saw the memo," no prosecutor or defense attorney ever brought it up in court, and according to Lano, "FBI Headquarters never made it public."

Interference and aggressive efforts by Nixon's White House to shut down the FBI's Watergate "locomotive" were immediate and substantial. It was gloves off—the bare-knuckle fight was on. Rumors of a concerted campaign of political "dirty tricks" against Democratic Party candidates created an atmosphere of fear and suspicion. In a political town like Washington, DC, refusing to knuckle under could torpedo careers and result in blacklisting, or worse—and worse had dark connotations.

The Watergate Complex and Howard Johnson Hotel—burglar's lookout

3

SATURDAY MORNING MASSACRE

Six weeks before the Watergate burglary, FBI Director Hoover died and Nixon appointed L. Patrick Gray Acting Director of the Bureau. Gray soon called a meeting of all the FBI Special Agents in the WFO because he wanted to "meet some real Agents." He looked out at the sea of Special Agents, all wearing white shirts—a Hoover requirement— and resembling a group of missionaries or Olive Garden staff minus the nametags, and announced, "Henceforth, you gentlemen are free to wear colored shirts." A resounding standing ovation met his dictum. Hoover's "white-shirt mandate" was at last lifted. Gray seemed off to a good start.

But Gray turned out to be tone deaf to FBI culture, and his inconsistent, vacillating leadership hampered our efforts to get to the bottom of Watergate. The machinations leading to the eventual downfall of Acting FBI Director L. Patrick Gray were multifold. He was a loyalist, and the naval culture he knew perpetuated a lockstep ethos of obedience and reverence. Questioning and dissent seemed unwelcome. There were leaders and there were followers. Up goes the information, down come the orders: predictable, comfortable, efficient, logical. Gray probably couldn't conceive that the president of the United States, in concert with his subordinates, would hatch a nefarious plan of serial burglary, bugging, and generally trashing the Fourth Amendment's safeguards against unreasonable search and seizure.

✫ ✫ ✫

Friday evening, June 23, 1972, one week into the investigation, Watergate Agents were telephoned at home and ordered to report to the WFO the next morning at 9:30 a.m. We would then proceed en masse to FBI Headquarters a few blocks away and meet with Gray. Saturday morning, June 24th, I reverted to wearing my "Hoover dress blues"—my best FBI blue suit, white shirt, conservative tie, and shined shoes. SAC Bob Kunkel seemed nervous as we assembled at the WFO in the Old Post Office Building. We soon created an unusual scene of twenty-seven serious-looking men in the same-style, monotone business attire walking down Pennsylvania Avenue en masse.

What could be awaiting us? I mused aloud, "Maybe we're going to get some kind of an award or commendation?" Other Agents fantasized about a possible group honor or special bonus for working this intricate, vexing case. Probably a long shot. We entered the Justice Department Building and proceeded to what had long been J. Edgar Hoover's office. It was now Gray's. Single-filing into the vast conference room, we came face-to-face with the Assistant Director in Charge of the Criminal Division, Charles Bates. He was standing rather gloomily, clipboard in hand, checking names. I'd never met Bates before, nor experienced a roster check for any previous meeting.

Bates and I spoke briefly, and he mentioned that we shared the experience of having worked in San Francisco. Hmm—how did he know that? Bates must have reviewed my personnel record, and surely every-one else's. This was unsettling. I proceeded into a big room, and we formed two arching lines around a huge, oval conference table outside Gray's inner office. SAC Kunkel was positioned close to Gray on one side, with Assistant Special Agent in Charge (ASAC) Ed Campbell, and our supervisor, John Ruhl, standing next to him. The assembled two dozen Agents filled out the balance of the oval on either side of the huge table. What happened next was unforgettable.

As L. Patrick Gray entered the room from his inner office, he looked angrily distressed, scowling like he'd just fumbled a football. Gray grabbed the rostrum firmly with both hands, looking determinedly focused and resolute. He then began an accusatory rant, a sweeping "chewing out" in an increasingly loud voice that boomed as emotional control slid from his grasp. His body began to sway and gyrate, his shoulders dipped and face reddened as he leaned and thrust his jaw for-ward. His formidable head looked every bit the navy captain, crowned with a gray crew cut. Earlier that week, confidential FBI Watergate information appeared in *Time* magazine by writer Sandy Smith. Gray was convinced the leak emanated from one of us.

"These leaks are coming from Agents of the Washington Field Office! I am sick and tired of you flap-jawed Agents. We are here today with this group to find out exactly which Agent or Agents leaked this information." His shouting escalated as he demanded, "The Agent or Agents who leaked information to Sandy Smith, take one step forward." Obviously I didn't move, nor could I imagine anyone else in the room taking responsibility, as I had full confidence that none of my peers would do such a thing. Street FBI Agents in Washington, DC, did not involve themselves in politics. We were investigators, nothing more.

When no one moved, Gray became incensed. "I demand that any Agent or Agents who leaked information to Sandy Smith or anybody else take one step forward immediately!" For several long seconds, no one dared budge. I was surprised to see SAC Kunkel begin to take one tentative step forward and attempt to speak. He was abruptly cut off by Gray's sharp, accusatory rebuke, *"Mr. Kunkel, did you leak the information?"*

Kunkel, a gentleman I respected, who probably wanted to say something in explanation or defense of his Agents, responded, "No, I did not."

Gray ordered harshly, "Then take one step back!" Kunkel complied and remained silent as the mood in the room darkened and soured. Witnessing my SAC, a high-ranking FBI official, demeaned outright in front of his Agents, I felt a sickening feeling sweep over me. We stood frozen in place as tension intensified. If Gray's prior sequence of demands, browbeating, and threats were not enough, the eruption that followed was from another planet.

Gray broke down, throwing himself into a total and complete fit of rage. He again vigorously grabbed the rostrum with both hands—his body and arms shaking, vibrating. His face was crimson as he screamed at the top of his lungs. "You...you will not fool me! I will get to the bottom of this! I am a former naval captain. I have commanded a nuclear submarine...I am a graduate of Georgetown University Law School! I have conducted many investigations in the navy, and I know how to conduct an investigation. I will find out who leaked the information to Sandy Smith. You group of men are nothing but a bunch of caterwauling individuals who do not have the guts or courage to come forward. If any of you ever appear before me again, in any context, I will fire you!"

I made a mental note to later look up "caterwauling" and discovered it means a bunch of wailing cats. The silence in the large conference room deepened. How much worse would this get? Gray turned to

Assistant Director Bates, standing to his right with clipboard in hand, looking rather embarrassed. Gray asked, "Do you have the name of every man in this room?"

Bates replied, "Yes, sir, I do."

Gray continued, "Well, make sure that you do. If any man in this group ever appears before me again...I will fire him!" Gray curtly ordered us "dismissed," pivoted, about faced, and strode back into his inner office. Stunned with disbelief, we just looked at one another and filed out of the room.

Walking back up Pennsylvania Avenue to our office at 12th Street, we shared our simmering anger. With each step, I could feel determination building. The "Saturday Morning Massacre" by L. Patrick Gray had a huge impact on everyone. Gray's debacle turned committed Agents into furious, fired-up, get-out-of-our-way Agents. His tirade had the effect of a pep talk. Instead of weakening our resolve, it achieved the opposite.

The C-2 Squad's bond was strengthened, inspiring us forward in the best FBI tradition to solve this case. It firmed up our determination and served as a catalyst to unify us in getting to the bottom of the Watergate case. Rather than receiving support from the top at FBI Headquarters, we felt betrayed. This deep, galvanizing anger was something none of us had experienced on this level in our Bureau careers. Gray's "shoot-from-the-hip" unsupported threats and accusatory, demeaning manner nudged him into the crosshairs of suspicion—was Gray himself the source of the leaks? Was it the C-2 Squad versus Hoover's successor?

Recalling this experience, I was amazed at how quickly and profoundly emotions came roaring back. In a recent conversation and email with my then-partner, Agent Paul Magallanes, I shared my strong recollections about the Saturday Morning Massacre. Paul wrote, "Gray called us 'yellow-bellied, sniveling Agents,' among other names. I had never, and not since, been talked to in such a manner as an FBI Agent, or as a human being. As I write this, I am reliving the insults, once again quivering from the anger I felt that day."

In spite of Gray, astounding information and intelligence about monetary payments and involvement emerged as we began interviewing CREEP employees and the people around the president. There was no doubt among the Agents working the case that the institution looming as our imposing target—the logical point from which the conspiracy was hatched and launched—was Nixon's White House supportive campaign apparatus. Nevertheless, FBI Headquarters was noticeably reluctant to OK coverage of key investigative leads, and without a complete, sequential investigative portrait developing and maturing, we were left with disparate, somewhat unrelated pieces. In effect, one couldn't make out the theme developing in the portrait.

Agent Angelo Lano's frustration grew. As agitation kicked into high gear, he paced and mildly ranted. Six days after the Saturday Morning Massacre, Friday, June 29, Lano fired a blistering teletype at the Bureau's highest echelons, demanding timely action. SAC Robert Kunkel refused to "sign out," or authorize, Lano's challenging missive. In response, Lano politely, but pointedly, confronted him, grabbed the text from Kunkel, and announced, "Watch this!" Lano signed Kunkel's initials at the bottom of the draft, drew a line, and placed his initials immediately beneath Kunkel's—"signing out" the fireball himself, thereby taking all responsibility. At FBI HQ, Associate Director Mark Felt read, but declined to initial, Lano's fireball, allowing it to simmer on Gray's desk in his absence.

Lano's memo prompted a follow-up meeting, where Acting Director Gray confronted a room full of key Watergate investigators and bosses. Gray once again allowed emotion to override judgment, authoritatively demanding to know who had the temerity to send the impolitic teletype. Lano answered up, stating that necessity required FBI Headquarters to be pushed beyond a nudge—he wasn't afraid to bulldoze the case forward.

4

THE MONEY TRAIL

"John, could you give me a hand with an interview?" Paul Magallanes, a fellow Agent on the C-2 Squad, stood behind his desk in the Old Post Office Building on a late Wednesday afternoon, July 19, 1972, a month after the Watergate burglary. He hailed from the South Side of Chicago and had an outgoing, engaging personality and a "hustler's attitude" (in a positive sense) toward working a case. Paul was a go-getter who pushed the boundaries, gently but relentlessly, and in the end effectively. He inspired trust that prompted reluctant witnesses to speak, and the FBI benefitted.

Other Agents in the office were finishing their shifts, doing paperwork, tying up loose ends, and chatting with each other about cases. I agreed to give Paul a hand with the interview, unaware that we were about to initiate and nail down a major break in the case. The large amount of cash carried by the Watergate burglars signaled there was some big, established money behind them. Our investigation hinged on finding, documenting, and following the money trail to link the Watergate burglars to its origin. If we were unable to locate and expose the source, our case would be substantially dependent on direct testimony. As yet we had no statements from any primary participant or peripheral player in the burglary, and the subjects in custody weren't signaling any willingness to cooperate.

Our bosses at the FBI, with the possible exception of Acting Director Gray, emphasized the importance of this investigation, giving it the highest priority with no resources spared, especially in the WFO, where Agents had been diverted from other responsibilities to the Watergate investigation. However, our resources weren't infinite, and the clock was ticking. If we could demonstrate, through tracing identified documents, that campaign donations were diverted by CREEP authorities to fund illegal operations, we'd have evidence of conspiracy to commit felonies.

Our goal became to interview all clerical, bookkeeping, and support personnel who worked for CREEP. This would be tension filled and difficult because they had been instructed not to cooperate with us. Ground rules were imposed. Interviews had to be conducted at CREEP offices or the White House, with a CREEP attorney present, which inhibited the forthrightness and candor of the witnesses. How could we surmount these obstacles, and would anyone have the courage to come forward?

Driving across the Potomac River toward the Key Bridge Marriott in Arlington, Virginia, Paul detailed background on the two women we were about to meet. Penny Gleason and Judy Hoback were employees of CREEP, the most logical organization under which the burglars would've operated. Penny grew up in a conservative Catholic family, and her parents were deeply committed Nixon devotees. When Penny participated in an initial FBI interview with Agent Paul Magallanes, held in the presence of a CREEP lawyer, she gave only "yes" and "no" answers. The morning after her interview, Penny initiated contact with the FBI. She confided, "I really have a lot to say, but I couldn't say anything in front of the lawyer."

Penny agreed to a confidential debriefing with Paul at a Holiday Inn. That meeting went seven hours, generating forty-seven pages of handwritten notes. She detailed a hurried destruction of burglary leader McCord's files, along with lying and deliberate misdirection of FBI efforts by CREEP bosses. Penny told Paul that her friend Judy Hoback, who was working as a bookkeeper at CREEP, was "really frustrated as to what's happening and has even more information." Judy and Penny were close friends who carpooled from suburban Maryland. Judy, a young widow with a baby to support, would be placing herself in a precarious position by stepping forward. Employees were being heavily pressured, even threatened, to keep silent. Nevertheless, she was ready to take the risk.

The Key Bridge Marriott, located in a section of Arlington filled with concrete high-rises so closely built together they looked like eggs in a carton, primarily served travelers on commercial and government business. Our meeting was to take place in the hotel cocktail lounge, which had no dedicated following—everybody was from somewhere else. There was virtually no chance our witnesses would be recognized, so it was an ideal location for our rendezvous. Paul introduced me to Penny, then Penny introduced us to her friend Judy, whose diminutive stature gave no hint of her towering moral sensibilities and courage.

I blended in, projecting a businesslike image—sitting down and ordering a Scotch and soda. We needed to create a relaxed, low-intensity atmosphere. That meant eye contact (but not too intense), projecting a sense of enjoying the hospitality, and carefully not exhibiting jitteriness or off-key behavior. Around a table we began our conversation casually with small talk about the day's news events.

This get-together was a screening—Paul and I were being tested and evaluated—and we moved forward only if we passed muster. Breaking the Watergate case might ride on whether we radiated trust. Our focus gradually shifted to the importance of Judy's knowledge about the case and her discomfort with the probable illegalities committed by her political bosses. I felt, but didn't show, a substantial degree of apprehension, so I was relieved when the conversation slipped into where Judy's interview should take place. Judy proposed that we leave and follow her to her Bethesda, Maryland, home.

The late evening's darkness and slacking commute traffic combined to provide embracing cover, but I was hyperalert for tails. We were very conscious of the real possibility of trailing cars, including counter surveillance by CREEP or the White House "Plumbers" operatives. The Plumbers, a clandestine investigations unit formed by Nixon in early 1971, was tasked with keeping a lid on press leaks and harassing political opponents. Plumber activities were led by previously mentioned E. Howard Hunt, an ex-CIA Agent and project manager, and G. Gordon Liddy, who formerly worked as an Assistant District Attorney in New York, as an FBI Agent, and as a Treasury Department employee. Liddy reported directly to Jeb Magruder, a former Nixon White House aide who became deputy director of CREEP in March 1971 under John Mitchell, Nixon's former attorney general. These guys were White House insiders and potentially very dangerous.

Paul and I followed Judy back to her Bethesda residence—classically American, small and homey, white clapboard, with a surrounding garden, white picket fence, and two matching dormer windows fronting the second story. Inside we cautiously inquired about personal and professional background to sketch out her basic identity and establish rapport. Quickly the conversation turned to the operational atmosphere at CREEP and her role and duties therein.

Judy handled the dispensing of funds, including cash, to support field operations. She had seen—and felt some responsibility for—the disbursement of thousands of dollars in cash for unlawful activities, including burglary. It deeply disturbed her. Judy detailed substantial, specific amounts of cash taken out of a large walk-in safe, in an atmosphere that suggested, "Just walk in and grab a handful... whatever you need." She had great recall of specific dates, people, and amounts. "Because I'm the accountant, I know what goes on here, where this money goes, and to whom it's paid: McCord and Liddy." She added that particularly large amounts went to Liddy.

At the time McCord was caught red-handed in the Watergate break-in, he was running a private security company and had been hired in that capacity by CREEP. The payment to McCord looked like the link between Nixon insiders and the Plumbers' "dirty tricks" campaign. It seemed cathartic and unburdening for Judy to set the record straight about the illegal and corrupt acts she witnessed and in which she'd been pressured to participate.

Judy described how much cash was dispensed to whom, and how CREEP funding supported the targeted burglary of the Democratic National Committee Headquarters at the Watergate. Her revelation of this slush fund was pivotal to tracing the money trail, providing direct eyewitness evidentiary testimony of money illegally flowing from campaign donations into the hands of Watergate burglars and Plumbers operatives—the financial linchpin of the entire investigation. By the end of the interview, at just past 3:00 a.m., we knew Judy Hoback, an ordinary American, was a true patriot who put country above self. It was shocking to hear her revelations but exhilarating to realize that we had this incredible break in the case.

The Smoking 302

Outside, Paul and I huddled. It was a warm, humid morning. I suggested we head straight to the office to record our findings. We dashed into the WFO to fill out our FD-302, the form on which we recorded all interviews, statements, and narratives of an investigation. Hours later, we were still drafting the 302 as other Agents began shuffling into the office to begin their workday. Around 9:30 a.m., we submitted our rough draft to the "Bureau steno," an office typist, and an hour later, we were reviewing the finished product. There it was: all nineteen single-spaced pages. The "Smoking 302" was a bombshell. Amounts, dates, people, the walk-in safe, piles of cash, inflows, and outflows were all documented. We were exhausted when we left around 11:00 a.m., but it was a good tired, knowing we'd conducted an interview of such monumental significance.

Penny Gleason's efforts were crucial in encouraging and supporting her friend to come forward, and, as Max Holland writes in *Leak*, "Hoback's revelations represented some of the most direct information about the links between the burglars and the Nixon reelection effort." Our interview with Judy, in retrospect, was a defining moment. Penny and Judy never received any medals, but they put it on the line for their country, exhibiting great strength and resolve. Don't bet against American sensibilities, conscience, and morality. A president and his minions did—and lost.

The Walk of Shame

Despite stonewalling, duplicity, unethical behavior, and illegalities of White House insiders, the system actually worked, and ultimately the bad guys got caught. The FBI and Justice Department operated under extreme duress, and there was always a risk politics would trump justice. Soon after our interview with Judy, the legal machinery began to churn. One by one, the men who worked for John Mitchell and CREEP traipsed into the WFO to be booked. Peering through an open door, down a worn marble walkway toward the arrested-subject processing area where common crooks were fingerprinted and photographed, I watched the motley crew of smooth, pedigreed, politically juiced men in expensive custom-made suits, gutless and unwilling to take a stand for what was right. Their actions would topple an American president. All it takes is a few people in positions of power to lose their ethical compass.

5

AHEAD OF THE CURVE

"John, did you see this?!" Paul Magallanes was clearly agitated. In his hand he angrily brandished *The Washington Post*. The front-page article of September 29, 1972, by Woodward and Bernstein appeared to contain direct quotes from our Smoking 302—the interview transcript from our meeting with CREEP accountant Judy Hoback. Paul proclaimed himself "shocked, amazed, and pissed." To us, it looked as if someone had handed the Smoking 302 directly to the two reporters. How could this happen? We were caught in a surging riptide, continually fighting unseen crosscurrents.

Unbeknownst to us, Carl Bernstein had visited and debriefed Judy Hoback in her home—two months after we'd interviewed her and written our Smoking 302. It seemed a dogged, determined Bernstein was following our trail. Woodward and Bernstein's ongoing public disclosures, precipitated by their covert informant Deep Throat, caused apprehension and tentativeness among potential cooperating witnesses. On the other hand, their investigative journalism bolstered public awareness of our case, spawning a national debate that brought force and legitimacy to our efforts. From my perspective, I couldn't imagine the leaker was an FBI Agent or official. Actually, I didn't speculate much on the leaks at all. On our level, the focus was on tasks at hand.

Decades later, deep into retirement, I learned the identity of the leaker. In 2004, Mark Felt, former FBI Associate Director and number-two man in the Bureau during Watergate, publicly admitted his role. It made perfect sense that Felt was Deep Throat. He had a reputation as an inner-sanctum master manipulator of long standing, with access and motives: personal (being passed over for promotion) and professional (exposing corruption to protect the Bureau and the integrity of the Office of the Presidency).

I'd first heard the name Mark Felt four years prior to Watergate, in September 1968. I'd been on my first FBI assignment for a few weeks in the Fort Worth Resident Agency when our efficient superclerk and office manager, James Black, excitedly entered our back room hideaway just before nine o'clock one morning as we were clandestinely drinking coffee and kibitzing (Hoover mandate: sipping java on the job was strictly verboten). I was to learn, respect, and appreciate that clerks in the FBI contribute mightily in a multitude of critical and vital support roles, collaborating with Agents in pursuit of sustaining the safety and protection of our country.

James exclaimed, "Golly gee, did you hear what happened in Oklahoma City?" We hadn't. He continued, "The SAC was at an NA (National Academy) gathering in Durant, Oklahoma, got into an argument with a chief of police's wife, and poured a drink between her breasts, down the front of her dress." Groans and disbelief all around, except from me. Almost bursting with pent-up, pivotal gossip, the office manager continued addressing an eager audience in a dramatic, chillingly concerned tone: "The Chief complained, and then Mark Felt arrived unannounced with three aides. They rented cars and secretly took affidavits. Felt walked into the SAC's office one morning at 9:00 a.m., gave him a check for his retirement contributions, fired him, then transferred a bunch of Agents." *Whoa.*

I was struck by the concerned reactions of the Agents and quivering voice of the clerk as he uttered Felt's name. Felt was FBI Associate Director, and intense fear and intimidation—big bill currency in Hoover's FBI—preceded his every field visit. Following the incident, reports had it that thirty Agents were transferred, including the eleven who accompanied the SAC to the ill-fated liaison event in Durant. Supposedly, everyone at Durant claimed they hadn't witnessed the drink-pouring incident, as each "happened to be in the men's room" at the time. Why was everyone so scared of Felt?

Hoover's Media

Understanding the development and evolution of Mark Felt requires knowing about his mentor. J. Edgar Hoover died only weeks before Watergate broke, after forty-eight years at the helm of the FBI. Hoover recognized and capitalized on the powerful influence of the media, crafting a national image of the FBI by schmoozing with select public personalities and using strategic leaks.

The FBI Headquarters tour ran for decades, dazzling Washington visitors with viewings of CSI-style lab work and briefings on gangsters and spies, culminating with an authentic G-man blasting away with a Thompson submachine gun. There's an old FBI story that in 1933, when George "Machine Gun" Kelly was being arrested, the unarmed gangster shouted, "Don't shoot, G-Men! Don't shoot, G-Men!" and the name stuck. On this once-favorite tour (currently unavailable), visitors saw no bored Agents slumped over gray, steel desks shuffling paper or staring at computer screens—they saw a select tourism spectacle engineered to craft a public image.

Hoover's relationships with media personalities influenced the FBI image in popular entertainment. Walter Winchell, using his deep New York City roots, became America's first radio gossip broadcaster, and as historian Marc Aronson notes, "Hoover put Winchell on a list of favored reporters who received the earliest and best stories of Bureau exploits: Winchell lavished praise on Hoover." Claire Bond Potter noted in *War on Crime* how "entrepreneurial journalists" were a crucial link for Hoover to shape public perception of the FBI.

Comic strips starring government Agents soon followed. In 1929, Hoover formed a long-term partnership with *Washington Star* reporter Rex Collier, who became, according to Potter, "the first newspaperman to be admitted behind the scenes of this closely guarded sanctum." Collier was the author of the *G-Man* comic strip. In 1933, *New York World Telegram* crime reporter Lou Weidman authored the comic strip *Special Agent J-8*. These men popularized the G-men for a national audience and made Hoover something of a celebrity.

James Cagney played a 1930s G-man, and in the mid-1950s, Jimmy Stewart starred in the movie *FBI Story*. A radio series emphasized both the Bureau's crime fighting and spy catching—it came on the air with dramatic music and a deep, sonorous voice, intoning, *"The FBI in Peace and War."* Columnist and show business reporter Ed Sullivan became an ally of Hoover's in radio journalism. Soon thereafter appeared a weekly TV series, *The F.B.I.,* featuring Inspector Lewis Erskine, played by Efrem Zimbalist Jr. and his junior assistant, Special Agent Colby.

Felt's Methods

When Watergate broke, Felt was a 30-year Bureau veteran who clearly understood the power of the media and how the FBI could use it. When disparate forces threatened the FBI's ability to probe deeply during an investigation, Felt worked with reporters to get the Bureau's message to the critical movers and shakers in our nation's capital—*The Washington Post* was unquestionably the most reliable conduit through which to reach those officials, and by extension, the American people.

As an FBI official, Felt would've been expected to maintain the highest secrecy about the Watergate investigation. He blurred, perhaps demolished, that requirement. At the same time, the FBI's Acting Director, L. Patrick Gray, was choosing loyalty to the president over ethical or lawful behavior. Felt's long-ranging duplicitous undercover role as Deep Throat could be seen as his way of protecting the integrity of the investigation against undermining assaults by the Nixon administration. Still, we experienced the negative fallout from Felt's leaks. Mere mention of his name still evokes strong emotions. While I never met him personally, his actions strongly impacted our work on the Watergate case. Why did this highly complex, controversial man generate such pointed, diverse opinions?

Felt's initial years as an FBI Agent were spent identifying, neutralizing, subverting, and arresting German spies and agents during World War II. Thomas Repetto's *American Policing* cites the FBI "taking the lead in arresting Nazi spies and saboteurs" as one of the two accomplishments that fueled J. Edgar Hoover's acclaim and made him a living legend. An expert in counterintelligence, Felt would have been schooled in double-dealing, enticing, threatening, blackmailing, misdirecting, and planting false stories. Might you become prone, or at least tempted, to test limits and push boundaries after years of such pursuits?

Felt climbed the FBI ladder, bringing fear, intimidation, and a touch of covert bullying to the job. He always delivered his messages personally, in staged, spy/handler manner. His effectiveness at intimidation highlighted his overall power of persuasiveness and even showed some brilliance. Agents aiming to reach the Bureau's highest leadership positions ascend within a rigid system. He was a veteran of multiple positions at FBI Headquarters, including chief internal enforcer, or "Inspector." The Inspection Staff—once nicknamed "Hoover's Enforcers" but also internally referred to as "The Goons" or "The Rats"—was a critical promotional touchstone. Fear and intimidation were their watchwords, almost slogans. Felt always seemed available for this work.

Felt maneuvered throughout Watergate to enhance his image in hopes of becoming FBI Director. In *Most Wanted*, Col. Thomas J. Foley of the Massachusetts State Police opined, "Deep Throat was hailed as an American hero for bringing down the Nixon Administration—until it turned out that he was actually Mark Felt, Associate Director, the FBI #2, who was furious that Nixon had passed him over as Director of the FBI, in favor of an outsider, L. Patrick Gray. So Felt did what FBI guys do. He used his inside information to retaliate, in this case by bringing down Nixon and his administration—anonymously, of course. It has nothing to do with patriotism. It was spite."

Foley wasn't the only one who suspected Felt's self-serving motivation. After Felt revealed that he'd been Deep Throat, SAC Jack McDermott of the FBI's Washington Field Office during Watergate said, "Felt was the Bureau's Benedict Arnold. Arnold betrayed his oath, his country, and his fellow citizen-soldiers to pursue his own ambitions. Felt did no less to the Bureau and his fellow Agents."

Crisis Management

Many years after Watergate settled, I learned that Felt had consistently pointed his finger at other Bureau officials and Agents as the sources of leaks. This created a firewall for Felt, deflecting suspicion from himself at the expense of our reputations and morale. Four decades later, Watergate Agents still harbor deep, bitter feelings. Felt's leaks also frightened witnesses vital to C-2's investigation, undermining the FBI Field Agents' credibility. Witnesses were scared. Some cooperating witnesses took the risk of working with the FBI, only to see their revelations blasted across the front pages of *The Washington Post*. We repeatedly reassured distressed witnesses, yet were unsure that we could really protect their confidentiality.

Despite the havoc Felt's leaking caused within the Bureau, there are other viewpoints. Felt seemed to believe that, unless somebody forced the issue, the FBI would never get to the bottom of Watergate. To the extent that his leaks may have bolstered the investigation and kept it alive long enough to reach its conclusion, some people view Felt as an American hero. Felt quickly identified the FBI's immersion in Watergate as a threatening crisis. Whether his crisis management was altruistic or part of a devious scheme to bring him the directorship is still open to debate. What mattered was that Felt refused to let the investigation falter.

As Deep Throat, the prime source and mentor-guide of Woodward and Bernstein's stories in *The Washington Post*, Felt kept the investigation in the news by "proactively plac[ing] a predicate story with a reporter with all the facts and the most favorable narrative thread...It allows you to get your viewpoint—your spin—into the story in a way that is credible." [Lanny J. Davis: *Crisis Tales*] In retrospect, Felt was ahead of his time acting as the FBI's crisis manager during Watergate, employing an offensive strategy (advocated by Lehane, Fabiani, Guttentag in *Masters of Disaster*) of "exposing the actions of those with unclean hands...The sooner you have the discipline to lead the disclosure parade, the better your position will be with the audiences who are evaluating you. In short, the story is coming—the question is whether you will be run over by the story, or whether you will be able to get in front of it."

Gray's Miscalculations

After Hoover's death in May 1972, Nixon appointed a new Acting Director, L. Patrick Gray. Lacking any relevant background or FBI experience, Gray additionally burdened himself by showing scant proclivity for learning Bureau functioning or establishing rapport with subordinates in Headquarters. He was aboard, but not on deck; thus Mark Felt's operational independence, power, and control actually ramped up. Gray spent his first several months on the job touring field offices, apparently in the mistaken belief that Field Agents cared. Field Agents are investigators and don't welcome attention from Headquarters. From their viewpoints, Gray's visits were pointless. Constantly out of the office, Gray didn't invest the time to build crucial trust via personal, face-to-face interaction with FBI HQ leadership. Citing his frequent absences from the real hub of power, Felt dubbed him "Three Day Gray" and eased into this leadership vacuum, keeping a fine-tuned, experienced hand on all the levers of the Watergate effort.

Gray hoped he could blame Watergate on the five guys caught in the act, as if they had just parachuted in from the blue. It was a while before he told Felt, "This could possibly be a political operation." Hmm—you've got the White House involved, CREEP involved, and White House Counsel John Dean monitoring every bit of information, including FBI reports. In fact, it was Gray who was giving Dean the reports. Gray either caught on a little late, was in denial, or was a co-conspirator—perhaps degrees of all the above.

Naval commanders go into damage control to save sinking ships in combat. When Gray faced Watergate, he reverted to his training and experience—compartmentalize, limit, contain the breech, and stay afloat. As Watergate FBI Agents, we were in attack mode, and our goals were operationally aggressive: open avenues of inquiry, broaden our scope, follow and exploit the "damage" to bring illumination, and "sink" or prosecute all persons, players, or actors criminally involved.

Gray seemed to vacillate and equivocate in his FBI leadership role and exercising his responsibilities. His inexperience, mixed loyalties, and political obligations undoubtedly pulled and propelled him into a hellish, simmering quagmire of Watergate crossfire. Gray trusted the White House, actively protected Nixon when he meddled, and—in a gross ethical lapse of possible criminal conduct—eventually destroyed relevant documents that he had secreted at his home in Connecticut. Gray was taking on water during the entirety of Watergate, even after he understood the White House was involved. He never effectively came to grips with the situation.

In a post-Hoover FBI burdened with inept top leadership, who better to capitalize on the power void than Felt? Felt's manipulation of the media was a continuation of Bureau tradition. When the Nixon White House tried to get the CIA to derail the Watergate investigation on grounds of national security, Felt selectively fed and nourished the media to arouse public awareness, making it difficult for Nixon to use this avenue to kill the investigation.

According to Max Holland's book *Leak*, Felt was concerned that Gray would not handle this case as aggressively as Hoover, and he constantly pushed Gray to "not sweep this thing under the rug." Felt told Gray that under no circumstances should the FBI back off from any investigation at the request of the CIA without forcing them to reveal completely the supposed threat to national security. Felt later said that he "never detected a reluctance on Gray's part to vigorously pursue this investigation," except that he "did feel that Gray was somewhat hesitant to look above rank-and-file (Nixon insiders)." When Felt suggested Gray personally go to President Nixon and say the FBI was receiving less than full cooperation from the White House staff and CREEP, Gray declined.

The Watergate saga challenged the FBI's operational credibility, integrity, and reputation. We were threatened by a collection of institutional heavyweights—the dominant political party and former Agents, operatives, and managers of the CIA and FBI—and from within by Gray. Meanwhile, John Mitchell, head of CREEP, was Nixon's former attorney general. Who knew where his connections penetrated?

C-2 was united in its determination to follow the case to conclusion. Case Agent Angelo Lano, who gave us insightful, gutsy, and focused leadership, was crucial to whatever successes the FBI experienced in Watergate. Everything pivoted around Lano, who positioned the investigation for eventual prosecution by coordinating with everybody who counted; identifying which avenues were important to pursue; determining timing, emphasis, and staging; and, of course, bearing ultimate responsibility for a "successful conclusion," whatever that would mean. He risked challenging Bureau hierarchy intransigence and stonewalling, enabling C-2 to plow forward.

You can't roll in the muck and come out clean. Duplicity and corruption leave everyone feeling soiled. The investigators of Watergate came away from the experience, to varying degrees, disillusioned, as did ordinary Americans. Although justice was served, there were no pats on the back, high-fives, or incentive awards. Commendations and honors are bestowed when circumstances are less uncomfortable. Navigating Watergate's dark voyage, we faced consistent, intense adversity—real and contrived—ambiguity, and immense pressure. Our motivation was to do the right thing, push relentlessly with fierce resolve, identify the rotten core, expose it, and excise it.

DAILY NEWS
NEW YORK'S PICTURE NEWSPAPER ®

FINAL ★★★★

15¢

Vol. 56. No. 39   New York, N.Y. 10017, Friday, August 9, 1974*   WEATHER: Partly cloudy, windy and mild.

NIXON RESIGNS

Acts in 'Interest of Nation,' Asks for End to Bitterness

Ford Will Take Oath at Noon, Kissinger Agrees to Stay On

Special 8-Page Pullout; Stories Start on Page 2

(source: Getty Images)

Part Two:

The Mission

Aug 1947

playing accordion and leading the band

1950

6

FUTURE PLANS UNKNOWN

San Francisco's Mission District: a diverse mix of architectural styles set among hills and a huge valley. Narrow passageways snaked in between main streets. Ours was about twenty feet wide and called Ames Alley. A hodgepodge of habitations housed assorted tradesmen, civil service workers, and their families, forming a happenstance landscape providing escape from, or pursuit of, other kids, and molding our characters as we grew up in the 1940s. As one of the biggest, tallest, and strongest kids, I often became default helper and young protector of others, a role that seemed to stick.

Baseball, played with a tennis ball, was the dominant game, and "strikeouts" a pitcher-batter duel. One weekend day, five of "us guys" were bouncing and throwing a tennis ball when a brand-new gray Mercury sedan slowly drove toward us. My younger brother Dick erratically threw the ball, which accidentally bounced off the car's fender—no damage done. A new neighbor who'd moved in a few doors down alighted from the car. He and his wife were quite the impressive couple, "dressed to the nines" as mother would say—a handsome business suit for him and strikingly stylish attire for her. Rumored to be a figure skater for *The Ice Follies*, she was already elevated to local celebrity status in Ames Alley.

The man, a young police officer and a member of an extended Irish family, berated my brother. His wife, quite upset, opened her door, bolted out and approached them. With an open hand, she struck my brother across the face with a violent slap. Dick screamed, turned, and ran crying into our nearby backyard. In short order, our Uncle Gene emerged from the lower flat, moving quickly. A tough fireman, Uncle Gene was formerly a helper, driver, and occasional sparring partner to heavyweight champion Max Baer and his brother Buddy in 1930s Oakland. Uncle Gene coached us all in boxing and had set up a speed bag in our basement, where we practiced and learned how to move about and defend ourselves, throwing quick, short punches from a proper stance.

Uncle Gene directly approached the off-duty cop. "Your wife better keep her hands off my family." Tension skyrocketed, leading to a mutual uncomplimentary exchange. My uncle, who must've figured he hadn't made sufficient verbal progress, uncorked a straight right punch, landing flush on the chin of the recalcitrant neighbor, who went down, flat on his back, not moving. The slap-happy wife screamed as she rushed to assist her fallen husband. My uncle's punch resonated with their family, because we never had any other problems with that group, who were rumored to be a tough bunch.

Uncle Gene's actions left quite an impression on me. They role-modeled how I was supposed to handle myself when confronting someone physically challenging the family. In Ames Alley you were expected to stand your ground, fight back, and not dwell too long about it—this was The Mission ethos. When I later faced a bullying attack, fight back I did, slugging it out. What triumph I felt as I struck my tormenter, and down he went as his father leaned out a window and yelled, exhorting his son repeatedly to "Kick him in the balls!" No Marquess of Queensberry rules here. A newfound awareness dawned: assertiveness, coupled with necessary "survival" confrontation—boxing and striking a punch—yields results.

Tables Turned

My defeated opponent soon became my pal. One evening he accompanied me to downtown San Francisco. Following my music lesson, we headed for Fifth and Mission Streets to catch a bus. It was tough going for me, as I carried a heavy accordion. Staggering toward us were three drunken sailors, much older and bigger than my friend and me. They mocked and challenged us. This was much more than the usual neighborhood threat. Fearful, we fled west on Mission Street toward Sixth, as the Navy Shore Patrol was usually on scene. I didn't make it to Sixth Street.

One of the sailors grabbed me from behind, spun me around, and, fists-up threateningly, backed me toward a large plate-glass window. Trapped, I set my stance and threw a punch, just like Uncle Gene, aiming for his chin. It struck full on, with a distinct crack, and the sailor sagged to the sidewalk. It was an instantly empowering feeling, deeply transformational: I realized I possessed the ability to fight back against the odds, actually control and reverse threatening situations, even prevail. Tables turned—lesson vividly reinforced.

As I grew taller and stronger, I continued to absorb Uncle Gene's lessons. Having the power to physically compete sometimes begets an obvious, yet limited range of reactions to life's challenges and problems. When you have a hammer, you want to handle every problem like it's a nail. Restrictive, reactive thinking dims the option of rationally filtered, multidimensional thinking. Acknowledgment dawned slowly of subtler, more enlightened, flexible options to life's meatier issues.

The Girls Next Door

My Ames Alley next-door neighbor, Patrick Ruane, was an Irish immigrant who departed County Galway at age seventeen for San Francisco and worked his way to the top of the Bay Area construction industry. Patrick oversaw the colossal build-out of San Francisco's Parkmerced development and the pump station of the Hoover Dam. I'd often accompany Patrick on ride-alongs in his pristine misty green 1947 Chrysler Town & Country, with its striking wood-paneled exterior doors, beautiful grill, chrome dashboard, and whitewall tires. I'd bring my accordion and perform as his opening act when he officiated at various civic gatherings. Many decades later, I would meet Patrick's great-grandson Brian Solon and together we would write this book.

John, his brother, his cousins, and the Ruane-Bisazza girls

"The girls next door": Patrick Ruane's granddaughters, Antoinette, Kathleen, Evelyn, Patricia, and Suzanne—mother of coauthor Brian Solon

Mission Interrupted

We'd never thought about locking our back doors until one afternoon our upper flat was burglarized by kids who stole a pair of binoculars. That's when my mom decided the evolving neighborhood was "no place to raise kids." Soon after, we moved across town to the far-western, fog-shrouded Sunset District, San Francisco's version of suburbia. Streets were neatly laid out on a grid (no alleys) bordering sand dunes which gently cascaded toward the Pacific Ocean. Unlike the Mission, it was stable and predictable.

My dad, John Henry, a career San Francisco police officer, stayed emotionally remote and selectively uncommunicative. We had little in common other than our bushy eyebrows, a physical trait passed on from my grandfather, who emigrated from Germany at age fifteen. Dad seldom offered praise or counsel, yet unleashed searing and barbed criticism—"How could you be so stupid?!" His demeaning character-izations cut deeply and haunted me for years, engendering a defeatist sense of self where it seemed I'd never measure up and success was be-yond my abilities.

Work gave me a feeling of accomplishment, a sense of self-worth, and a degree of independence in having my own money. Once I started working, I never really stopped. Unlike my home life, the workplace was an ego-building, defined environment where my efforts were ac-knowledged, praised, and rewarded. There were promotions and op-portunities given if you performed well. Work was therapy for me—an escape and opportunity for growth and achievement.

When I was twelve, my nine-year-old brother and I set up a roadside apple stand in Sonoma County and made more than a little spare change. In the resort area of Rio Nido on the Russian River, about seventy miles north of the Golden Gate, I spent most of my thirteenth summer work-ing two jobs as a pin-setter in a bowling alley and stocking soft-drink bottles on ice at a concession stand. During a few Octobers I did heavy farm labor, picking walnuts in Cupertino.

Approaching age 13, I wanted to stay in the neighborhood and go to Mission High School, like many of my local friends. Mom intervened and directed me to attend Lowell, a top-tier San Francisco public school where confident kids, encouraged by parents and/or fueled by ambition, seemed to have a swagger and knew how to get things done. The student council somehow convinced entertainer Sammy Davis Jr., emerging young superstar and featured performer with *The Will Mastin Trio*, to entertain at our pep rallies. He was phenomenal singing, tap dancing, and soloing on the drums.

For three summers in the mid-1950s, I worked outdoor laboring jobs—collecting garbage, truck driving, and lifeguarding—in the Sierra Mountains, just outside Yosemite near Hetch Hetchy reservoir at Camp Mather, a family vacation destination frequented by cops, firemen, and a diverse spectrum of middle-class San Franciscans willing to sacrifice a bit of comfort for a reasonable price.

In 1953, at age sixteen, I spent the summer working full-time in a machine shop as a production worker in Emeryville. This experience taught me that I absolutely did not want to spend a lifetime in front of a lathe grinding metal, eating lunch with "the guys" when the bell rang, dwelling on "stuff" in gross, profane terms. There was a dulling, almost crippling "sameness" defining each day. On payday, workers lined up outside the foreman's office, where he individually handed you a check. During breaks I'd flip open a window and gaze out down San Pablo Avenue toward Oakland thinking, "I don't know where I'm going, but I'm never coming back to this place."

With competitive swimming and water polo skills, I lettered on my high school swim team, then earned Red Cross and YMCA certifications as a master lifeguard and water safety instructor. Those qualifications provided me continuous part-time employment, and years later when I was an enlisted man in the army, I found myself reassigned from clerical trainee in an infantry outfit to a full-time lifeguard spot at a small, out-of-the-way army camp in the hills just behind Hearst Castle on the California coast, Camp Hunter Liggett. Despite having amassed a wide collection of life experiences by age eighteen, my vision of a future was virtually nonexistent. The statement alongside my graduation yearbook picture was a vague, uninspiring, but true, "Future Plans Unknown."

Jarring Realities

With one of the world's greatest natural harbors, San Francisco was a huge navy town, the gateway to the Pacific Theater during World War II. Tucked in the safe confines of the quiet, manicured Sunset District, I envisioned enlisting in the navy for adventures on the high seas, departing beneath the Golden Gate Bridge perched high on the deck of a massive ship.

Gladys and John H.Minderman (dad spelled our last name with one 'n')

My mom, Gladys, directed me to explore collegiate alternatives. She was born into a large, hardscrabble "ranching" family in the Sacramento Valley, and her parents produced a lot more kids than wealth and prosperity. Her Irish, French, and English heritage bestowed her with handsome features, shiny black hair, and a feisty demeanor, which she generously passed along to me. She was direct and determined that I get a good education. I took the last entry examination to San Francisco State University, confident that I would flunk it and then spend a few months in junior college before drifting away to the deep blue sea. Returning home one afternoon, I saw Mom smiling, holding aloft a penny postcard, trumpeting that I'd passed the SF State entry exam.

While it wasn't exactly sailing the South Seas, SF State was located on a brand-new, beautiful campus, adjacent Parkmerced. S.F. State's modest fees of $12.25 per semester for up to 18½ undergraduate units and laid-back atmosphere compelled me to push back my navy aspirations for a few more months. First-rate professors taught an array of fascinating social science and history courses, and I dove in, doing well. I loved the half-unit recreational PE classes, especially badminton, and competing on the water polo team, where we won the Far Western Conference championship.

On the SF State JV baseball team, I played outfield and sometimes catcher. At one of our batting practices, the coach threw me a couple of fast pitches, which I blasted 375 feet over the fence each time. Unbeknownst to me, Eddie Lake, a former Pacific Coast League third baseman for the San Francisco Seals and scout for the Boston Red Sox, had shown up seeking possible prospects. After practice, Lake introduced himself and offered me a position on the Stockton Class D minor league team and a $500 signing bonus. I knew I could hit with power and "had an arm" but was shocked to be considered good enough to go pro at any level. The potential opportunity of a lifetime was right there in front of me, but my self-doubts prevailed. I thanked him for his offer and declined.

Spirit of the Radio

SF State's Radio and TV Broadcasting program was a major department on campus, with numerous successful graduates in the industry and internships available at local stations. It was a golden opportunity to study within an emerging, rapidly growing professional discipline I found fascinating. I'd have a real chance to prosper. I'd grown up listening to radio shows like *Red Ryder, Jack Armstrong—The All-American Boy*, and *Superman*—"faster than a speeding bullet" who could "leap tall buildings in a single bound." *Dragnet's* Sergeant Friday, with Jack Webb's narration ("Just the facts, ma'am"), was my idol. On TV, one of my favorites was *The Lineup*, a groundbreaking dramatic series about San Francisco police in the 1950s.

San Francisco had long been a hotbed of creative radio broadcasting, going back to the 1920s. It was on San Francisco's Telegraph Hill, 202 Green Street, September 7, 1927, where inventor Philo Farnsworth transmitted the world's first TV image and announced to his stunned lab assistants, "There you are—electronic television!" When I mentioned SF State's Radio and TV program to my dad, he strongly disapproved, dismissively saying, "You can't major in that. That's not a real profession. You need to pursue something solid, like school teaching." I reluctantly heeded dad's mandate to become a teacher, but needed a backup plan.

A Certain Mystique

Over the course of my dad's forty-year career in the San Francisco Police Department (SFPD), he began directing traffic, then transferred to being a motorcycle cop on Van Ness Avenue, eventually landing on a cushy regulatory detail responsible for taxicab oversight. He was well liked, and he seemingly thrived and enjoyed the routine, noncriminal elements of policing, avoiding confrontations and arrests—the very areas of police work I'd eventually find most challenging and fulfilling.

John Henry Minderman with SFPD Lt. Nels Stohl and Off. Charlie J. Haster

Amid other academic pursuits, I elected to explore my options and took *Introduction to Criminology* at SF State, taught by Professor George Outland, a tall, heavy-set, bald, perpetually perspiring teacher. Three SFPD officers were in my class. On our first midterm, Outland announced he didn't feel it necessary to monitor the test, since there were

police officers present, and left the room, concluding "the honor system" would suffice. As I sat in front taking the test, I heard talking
behind me and turned to see the three "guardians" huddled together
around cutout pages from our textbook, looking up answers. Cops conspiring to cheat—disparaging themselves, their department, and profession—an eye opening experience.

Sworn In

In preparation for the Patrolman's Civil Service examination, I took
courses at Quigley's Coaching School. Tuition was 50 cents a week.
Retired Deputy Chief Quigley personally taught each class in his dirt-
floor basement, with long, wooden benches and tables. He did a great
job, and to my father's chagrin, I passed the local Civil Service Police
Test at #23 during my senior year, securing a spot on the eligible list for
Police Academy appointment. On July 1, 1959, after graduating from
SF State with a bachelor's in social science, I was sworn in as an SF police
officer on the interior steps of the old Hall of Justice on Kearny Street,
bordering Chinatown. The oath was administered by Chief Thomas J.
Cahill, branded "The Lion" for his blond mane and fierce look.

The Police Academy, located west of the middle of Golden Gate
Park, featured a curriculum with lots of dos and don'ts, elementary
criminal law, basic investigatory procedures, report writing, organized
exercising, marching, and even how to use a handheld Geiger Counter
to measure radiation, just in case the Big One—an atomic bomb—
dropped. We weren't told how to actually survive the Big One so we'd
be able to use the instrument. I imagined myself as a cartoonish burned
stick figure, technically challenged, situated atop Twin Peaks, survey-
ing the rubble below, taking a Geiger-counter reading. At that point,
who'd care? It was emblematic of the attempts of public-service agencies to combat a Cold War terror far beyond their control.

Of the thirty-four members of the 87th recruit class, about one-fourth were college graduates. Many in the class mirrored me: without direction, in search of a "soft landing"—a job with good pay and benefits, or at least a few productive years while one scanned the career horizon contemplating viable exit strategies.

The Floater

After graduation from the Academy, it was on to Northern Station, known as "Company E," or "The Big E"—one of SF's roughest, most diverse police districts. It encompassed the western part of the Tenderloin, with hustlers of every stripe, parolees, probationers, single-occupancy hotels, bars, cafés, and places for every element to hang out. Also within our district, in stark contrast, were wealthy Pacific Heights, the trendy Marina District, and the volatile Fillmore ("The Moe"). Commercial strips sandwiched in between distinct subdistricts marked out informal boundaries.

As a night-patrol, rookie officer, I'd be working without a permanent assignment: a "floater" (a term, I recalled, that also meant "a body in the bay"). My days and nights were packed with activity. While working in the SFPD full time, I took graduate courses to qualify as a teacher and eventually did student teaching during the day. Being California state-credentialed would enable me to instruct in the social sciences and history statewide up through the junior college level.

Pursuing two careers simultaneously was fatiguing, and I barely managed to grab a bit of sleep on a hard, narrow, locker-room bench during quick breaks. I'd have to make a choice. Police work seemed adventurous, mysterious, unpredictable, spontaneous, even dramatic, with a certain mystique—the element of the "hunt." Wide-open opportunities existed to initiate and engage in entrepreneurial "on view" criminal encounters. The whole package was contagious.

San Francisco Police Department review at City Hall—October 31, 1925

San Francisco Police Department 87th recruit class—October 5, 1959

7

POLICE WISDOM

"Remember, men: You either got somethin'—or you got nothin'.
If you got nothin'—don't try makin' somethin' out of it.
Sergeant, dismiss the men."
—Lt. Stephan J. Flahavan

My cautious driving pointedly annoyed veteran officer Lloyd Hill. "Listen, John, when you're the law, you've got to drive like the law!" Style, presence, and image projection count in policing—the thin buffer line between order and chaos. You represent power and control. In the face of confusion, threat, intimidation, and confrontation, you must act and prevail. Inactivity or retreat isn't an option. If police lose control of a situation, appeal for assistance is ultimately directed to the National Guard or Army. Help might come much too late. You must move with confidence and push the boundaries—be bold.

When I walked a foot beat, the only forms of communication were a whistle and a blue steel telephone box situated on top of a freestanding pole or attached to a utility pole. Call boxes were placed every few blocks, opened with a special brass key, and contained a phone that connected to an operator who routed your request. Footmen checked in every two hours. If someone "missed a box," bosses sent everyone searching, as we walked alone, carrying a 4-inch, 6-shot, .38-caliber revolver with reloads, a whistle, flashlight, and pocket club. It could get rather lonely out there, and with the San Francisco fog rolling in, it was damp and bone-chilling cold.

In a squad car we had a radio, but as soon as we alighted to engage or handle a call, we were on our own. The cars were stripped-down, six-cylinder, basic sedans, with a shotgun vertically locked into the dashboard, very little power, no special handling modifications, and for many years, no heaters—cold duty, even in a car. On the positive side, when we ended a shift, took off our uniforms, and departed, we generally left behind our work worries and concerns. There were few long-term issues. Our responsibilities on patrol were defined, but the situations weren't—anything could happen. We were virtually free of supervision, rarely seeing a sergeant after roll call. This gave lots of latitude, so long as we "hit our boxes" or "handled our runs."

Midnight shifts we'd cruise without destination, floating through city streets. Alternately you could aggressively "crank it up," seeking out "on view" encounters with criminals in places where they were skulking about, likely contemplating working crimes. You were an isolated, mobile island—every interpretation or reading of a situation was yours alone. You might initiate action but were always wary, alert to shifting cues, responding to spontaneous menaces and threats.

Both quality and number of arrests in this enforcement built one's reputation and represented an important informal scorecard of an officer's worth, defining him as a "real cop." This process honed your capacity to filter inputs, as described by Francis P. Cholle in his book *The*

Intuitive Compass: "A gut feeling—or a hunch—arises before a person becomes conscious of it; it can enrich their ability to make a decision. It is a sensation that appears quickly in consciousness (noticeable enough to be acted on if one chooses to) without us being fully aware of the underlying reasons for its occurrence."

Timing is critical in policing. Survival depends on reading the scene, thinking and acting fast, and staying mentally and physically ahead in every phase of an encounter. A decision-making cycle—"The Boyd Loop"—was identified by Air Force Colonel John Boyd based on his observations of combative dogfights between MiGs and US fighter pilots over Korea: "[t]ime is the dominant characteristic in outsmarting any opponent, by making appropriate decisions quicker than an adversary, a concept that favours mental agility over brawn. The speed with which the process can be undertaken often marks out the better commander, or command team." [Peter Caddick-Adams: *Parallel Lives: Monty and Rommel*]

San Francisco in the 1960s was a hotbed of social and political upheaval hearkening back to the freewheeling days of the Barbary Coast. Since its birth as a city, SF played stage to contentious clashes, including the General Strike of 1910 ("The Birth of Muni"), the Preparedness Day Bombing in 1916, and the Waterfront Strike of 1933. Instability seems imbedded.

For a young man, the actual street work was both stimulating and very dangerous. An officer is always one comment, one look, or one perceived slight away from violence. Keeping the peace required informed perception and real acting skills. Occasionally, that short pocket club made a statement when displayed, and if necessary, slowed aggressors when used. Some of the most fascinating experiences I had as a patrol officer occurred at night in high-crime areas. The job was awash in challenging and even hilarious episodes.

As a fresh-faced, twenty-two-year-old police rookie, I headed onto my first midnight watch walking a beat in this simmering cauldron with my mission of maintaining order—by always taking the "proper police action."

It's a Gun

The Gangway was most definitely a second-tier bar, possibly edging lower, frequented by marginal part-time workers, felons on parole, and individuals on local probation—not a joint for enjoying cocktails before attending the SF Opera. The bar was a likely place to find someone involved in or hovering around illegalities, and it would be my first stop on a midnight tour. In the surrounding neighborhood, a slightly watered-down western extension of San Francisco's infamous Tenderloin, menace was almost tangible.

I walked in, hesitated momentarily, and surveyed the scene. True to the establishment's moniker, its layout was a long, bulging, narrow passageway, with very little room between the bar and opposite wall. As I walked toward the rear to talk with the bartender, I passed a woman and two men standing with their backs against the bar. Sidestepping slowly past the woman, I thought I heard her whisper, "It's a gun."

In milliseconds my mind raced. "Did I really hear that? Why would she say that? Wait, does one of these guys have a…?" Moving by the next man who was facing me, my eyes lowered as his right hand was sliding diagonally inside his jacket toward his belt. We locked eyes, his face showing no emotion as I grabbed his hand and pressed it against his belly, feeling the rectangular butt of a massive semi-automatic pistol.

Boyd's Loop in action: I ordered him, "Don't move!" Next I told the surrounding patrons to step aside as I removed a cocked .45 from his waistband. Turning him around, I ordered him to place his hands on the bar. With his .45 semi-auto in one hand, and with my other hand firmly grasping his coat collar, I shoved him forward forcibly to show who was in control. For a few seconds, I was flummoxed. What to do now? I recalled that training maxim: always take the "proper police action." I just had to figure out what that was in these circumstances.

Out of the corner of my eye, I saw the bartender nearby, watching closely. I slid the cocked .45 down and across the bar toward the bartender and ordered him to secure and control the weapon. He placed his hand over the gun on the bar, out of reach of the suspect. I then ordered the suspect to place his hands behind his back, as I continued to firmly press him forward across the top of the bar. He didn't resist as I cuffed him up quickly, ensuring relative security.

Turning to the bartender, I said, "Move toward the phone, keep the gun under control on the top of the bar, and call the police. Tell the operator I'm the 'beat man,' and I have a prisoner under arrest. Say that I need a radio car quickly, but it's not an emergency." Moments later, to my relief, two officers from the Northern 4 car—Gus Stremme and Waldo Jackson—entered the bar.

We learned the gun-carrying suspect was on parole after serving a stretch for manslaughter at San Quentin. It's doubtful he was pulling the pistol for mere display or a hold-up robbery. He was, I believe to this day, intending to shoot me in the back. I'm ever grateful to the woman who so softly voiced those three words, "It's a gun." If disbelief prevailed and I'd hesitated another fraction of a second, the convicted killer would've drawn his loaded gun, and I'd have been toast—with one of the all-time briefest beat officer careers in the history of the SFPD.

Puff Puff

Officer Waldo Jackson and I drifted slowly east on Geary in the Northern 4 car on a beautiful, sunny, windless Sunday afternoon. Wally was a low-key, soft-spoken, chain-smoking, former minor-league ball-player in his midthirties. He had a wicked chuckle and nothing seemed to faze him. I was looking forward to learning from his wisdom on this swing shift.

Suddenly the radio crackled alive with a call for Northern 4. We were assigned to "California and Polk...a '418'—proceed to a bar to handle a fight in progress." Wow, real policing involving violence. For a twenty-two-year-old rookie, it doesn't get much better. Wally continued at moderate speed east on Geary, right past Polk. What happened? He should have turned left on Polk. I pointed this out. "Wally, you missed the turn; we've got to go north on Polk!"

Wally, taking occasional puffs on his cigarette, casually blew smoke out the window. "This way, by the time we get there, John, they'll either be gone or too tired to fight." Disappointed at missing the action, I tried to encourage Wally to proceed directly to California and Polk, but to no avail. True to Wally's prediction, when we finally arrived at the location, nobody was there—at least, nobody fighting.

When Wally wrote up the call at the station later, in the middle of the "Lab 48 Report," a single-page, yellow form used for summarizing action encountered in radio assignments, Wally wrote in big letters "GOA" (Gone on Arrival). As an eager young rookie, I was always looking to experienced officers for nuggets of what I thought of as Police Wisdom. Wally's seemed to be "Always handle your assignments, just don't be too quick to place yourself in unnecessary jeopardy." I wasn't too sure I wanted that particular nugget.

The Usual

Joe was a strong, barrel-chested, cigar-smoking, regular beat man who pulled his hat down so low his forehead was invisible and eye contact was minimal. Looking at him, one viewed a questionably hospitable face with a stubby cigar between clenched teeth. I was a rookie officer filling in for Joe's regular walking partner.

Our beat, the heart of the Fillmore, was lined with businesses offering drinking, diversion, and it seemed, happenstance illicit gambling. Friendly, smiling, scantily clad women wandered the area. During the wee morning hours, our area was notorious in police circles for crime, confrontation, violence, and all varieties of mischief. Threatening street crowds brewed as quickly as instant coffee. "Community Relations" was dawning as a watchword of police departments in the early 1960s. As walking officers, our job was to keep the peace as best we could, but in all circumstances, maintain control to ensure street incidents didn't spiral into multiple violent actions spurring mob behavior.

More than a few times, we came very close to that nebulous, ill-defined "tipping point," where a threatening crowd of as many as twenty to thirty people would mill around us, gesturing, yelling, even taunting, as we quickly tried to reach a blue police call box while simultaneously trying to subdue and calm a violent, resisting, drunken arrestee in custody. "Taunting" singled you out and earned you a ride in the Paddy Wagon.

Joe knew me from working out in the local Central YMCA weight room. As we motored out to the Fillmore in Joe's personal car, we parked near the intersection of Webster and Fulton, where a local bar known as *Kelly's Club* prospered. We entered and proceeded directly to the rear, nodding to some of the patrons. Moving aside a thin curtain, we found a table and a couple of chairs. Joe motioned to me to have a seat. The bartender appeared and asked, "What'll it be?"

"The usual," replied Joe.

The bartender looked at me, and caught off guard, I mustered up, "Make it the same," having no idea what I had just ordered. Minutes later, the bartender returned carrying a circular tray containing ten shot glasses, each holding an ounce and a half of bourbon. He placed five in front of Joe and five in front of me. So this was "the usual." One glass at a time, I began sipping my bourbon. By the time I finished my third glass, I was becoming woozy and unsettled. After the fifth, I definitely "had a little heat on" (a.k.a. *noticeably under the influence*). Needless to say, Joe's occasional program of "The Usual" couldn't become my program and would not become a part of my routine. It wasn't uncommon for bartenders to offer drinks to police while the officers were working—this seemed to be a part of the fabric of The City. Drinking on duty was accepted and commonplace, which generally came as a shock to rookies.

The Cable Car Village

On a midnight watch, Beat 5's Geary Street, west of Leavenworth, was my venue. It was a raucous, middling commercial strip bordering the fringe of the Tenderloin—a slow-simmering, alcohol-fueled, and prostitute-inhabited minor-league underworld. All manner of hoodlums, borderline denizens, and thugs slithered around Geary. A continuous hint of illicit activity, drinking, gambling, and drugs prevailed, and deals of every kind could be struck. My beat was a slightly less animated version of this district, with local bars colorfully named *The Tahitian Hut*, *Ralph's Ha-Ra*, and *The Gangway*, where, three months earlier, my first night on patrol was nearly my last.

Walking the area, curiosity spurred my decision to turn north and check out a few blocks on Hyde. A steep uphill climb brought me to California Street, where I noticed a small bar, the *Cable Car Village*, tucked unobtrusively beneath a three-storied, bay-windowed building of flats. It neared 1:30 a.m., and I decided to check out this new little find, walking slowly across the cable car tracks on California Street toward the establishment. I casually meandered through the front door and ran my eyes down the length of the bar. Something seemed unusual: no women present. Near the back of the place, a jukebox fronted a small dance floor occupied by three male couples dancing with each other. Could it be? I'd heard such places existed.

The record needle scratched loudly, and the music fell silent. Dancing activity came to an abrupt halt as all eyes turned and fixed upon my uniformed presence—the bartender and all patrons frozen in place. I knew it was a violation of our local Municipal Code "for persons of the same sex to dance with one another," yet I was too taken aback to think what "proper police action" might be. Slowly I backed toward the front door and exited.

Later that morning, I was due to meet my patrol sergeant. Making a mental note to advise him of my findings at the *Cable Car Village*, I continued wandering. At 3:00 a.m. I met my Sergeant in front of the Tahitian Hut, featuring one of San Francisco's most captivating tavern exteriors, depicting exotic, South Seas scenes etched into the concrete facade. The Sergeant was a herculean man who, in his free time, supposedly enjoyed swimming at Ocean Beach through the forbidding riptide currents around Seal Rocks, recorded our visit in his sergeant's book. As he took notes, I mentioned, "Earlier tonight I walked up Hyde and checked out a place—the *Cable Car Village*." The Sergeant ceased writing and noticeably tensed.

I added pertinent detail. "You know, Sergeant, I walked in and there were no women at all, just guys. I noticed three male couples dancing in the rear, and I know it's a violation of our Municipal Code (MPC) for people of the same sex to be dancing in a bar." The code was awash with obscure prohibitions, selectively invoked against recalcitrance or agitated, aggrieved citizens who had the temerity to threaten or rudely challenge the police. It was a cop's powerful stealth tool.

The Sergeant fixed his gaze on me and responded in an apprehensive tone, "Well, it is." I wasn't sure if he was referring to the dancing violation, but he quickly added that the bar was, "in fact, a homosexual hangout." He insightfully followed up, "You know, we don't do anything about it, because if anything happens involving them, we know where to find them."

The light bulb went on. "Aha!" I mused, "This must be another nugget of Police Wisdom. We selectively do or don't do things, because it gives us options and control." I responded, "Makes sense." At last, I was catching on. I grasped the wisdom of the sergeant's *"Do nothing and find 'em"* strategy. Police Wisdom could now actually start becoming part of my work. I was maturing. The sergeant looked more relaxed as we left one another's presence, and I was not to see him again, nor was I ever again assigned to Beat 5.

Fast forward to a few months later. Lurking like a dark shadow was my "Selective Service" status, or "The Draft." No eligible male eluded military service. Two years of "ground pounding" in the infantry was my horizon if I waited for the Army's call. Seeking another soft landing, I looked into the 91st Division—within which existed a small subunit, "special services," focused on recreation—headquartered in San Francisco's Presidio.

My quest led to a meeting with Sergeant Nichols at his SF Fort Mason office, housed within leftover WWII wooden barracks, with scores of Singer sewing machines stacked haphazardly around its perimeter. Nichols, who successfully balanced his Army career with side work as a Singer sewing machine salesman, wore a uniform shirt with three stripes and two "rockers" below, denoting a rank of Staff Sergeant. He was receptive to my pitch regarding my qualifications for service in his Army unit—which required only six months "active duty" training, twice-monthly evening "meetings," and two week "summer camps" for several years, to fulfill my total obligation.

After enduring Army basic training, I was assigned to Fort Ord, near Monterey, to join the "Remington Raiders"—whose moniker derived from their "weaponry" of choice: the Army's standard-issue Remington typewriters—working diligently to polish my typing skills and acquire basic clerking abilities. On my early morning break about 10:30 a.m., I took the *San Francisco Chronicle* newspaper out of my rear pocket and began scanning the front page where my eyes flew to a story about cops being arrested for "shaking down a bar." Alongside the text, I saw a picture of the Sergeant in handcuffs, alongside the other regular beat man, also cuffed up. They'd apparently been extorting the *Cable Car Village* for payments so the club could stay in business and cops would "look the other way." So much for Police Wisdom.

The Double-Back

Cops who were on the force for many years had the opportunity to work the day watch (8:00 a.m. to 4:00 p.m.), maintaining a schedule like the majority of working people. They could almost have a "normal" life. The rest of us worked alternate weeks of evening shifts (4:00 p.m. to midnight), then midnight shifts (midnight to 8:00 a.m.). Every other week, we changed from midnight shift to evening shift. Thus, once every two weeks we would leave work at 8:00 a.m. after an intense all-night shift, have only 8 hours off to catch up on sleep and life, then have to report back to the station at 4:00 p.m. and begin another eight-hour shift until midnight—the "double-back"—working 16 hours within 24. On the swing shift leg of a double back, cops were often out of sorts, inattentive, and irritable.

To cope with this affliction, some foot patrolmen were fortunate enough to acquire keys to the side-access fire door of the Royal Theater on Polk Street near California. When fellow officer Gene Harriman presented me with my own key, I felt a special brotherly acceptance. On future double-back shifts, I could occasionally grab some much-needed sleep on the comfy couches in the theater's mezzanine. A public pay phone was conveniently within earshot, providing a handy point of contact in case the station duty officer needed to interrupt my nap for an urgent matter on my beat.

One night at about 10:15 p.m., while walking a beat on the double-back, I entered the Fox Theater on Market Street to escape creeping fatigue and get off my feet for a few minutes. Resting within the unbelievably comfortable seats, I was lulled to sleep by the movie soundtrack. Abruptly I was awakened from my spontaneous sweet slumber at 12:12 a.m. when the theater's house lights went on. "Oops, I'm in big trouble: twelve minutes overdue in reporting off at the station." Realizing the entire station was likely trying to find me, I hustled to the pay phone. Thankfully two veteran officers answered my call and came to pick me up. Disdainfully one muttered, "Get in back." Northern Station's Lieutenant George Sully mildly rebuked me, but I think deep down he understood.

On another occasion I encountered unwanted attention while resting in the deserted balcony of the Alhambra Theater on a Sunday evening double-back watching Elizabeth Taylor in *Butterfield 8*. My jacket rested across my lap, covering my gun and cuffs, and my police dress-blue shirt with black tie and industrial-width black suspenders were visible—yet unrecognized—by an overly happy guy who came bounding up the stairs, zeroed in on me, rapidly approached my aisle, then made a beeline for the adjacent seat and situated himself uncomfortably close. To his chagrin, I slowly removed my jacket from my lap, offering plain view of my gun, cuffs, and police star. Mr. Friendly's eyes widened, then he quickly jumped up and raced to the stairs, taking them two at a time.

Double Vision

On a midnight watch, I was on the back of the "Paddy Wagon," a large van with bench seating on each side of the interior and no door on the back. This vehicle was designed for securing and removing arrestees. An officer stood on a heavy steel step, hanging onto long bars on either side, or onto a horizontal one on top, resembling a scene from the Keystone Cops. The wagon cruised around picking up anyone sitting or lying about, keeping drunks, druggies, and riff-raff upright and vertical.

We wound up being dispatched about 2:00 a.m., along with several radio cars, to a fight in progress outside a hotspot bar, which catered to a mixed clientele of young to middle-aged, upwardly mobile patrons, located on the upper end of Fillmore Street bordering upscale Pacific Heights. On scene, people were duking it out on the sidewalk. I hopped off the wagon and waded in, confronting a large, muscular man crouched in a boxer stance, ready to punch. My uniformed presence made no difference to him—he wanted to fight. As we circled one another, he warned that he was a professional fighter and added I'd better not "mess" with him (although the word he chose wasn't "mess"). Verbal cautioning, or ordering him to "cease and desist," seemed unlikely to work.

Assessing the situation, I figured that if I was going to hit a professional boxer, I'd best make sure to hit hard. In close, I saw an opening and instinctively set my feet, preparing to quickly pivot my arm, shoulder, and hips as I delivered a slashing, fist-first left hook, with just enough follow-through. It landed flush on his jaw-line, just like Uncle Gene taught me back in Ames Alley, with an audible crack. He reeled backward and dropped smack to the sidewalk.

Some weeks later, I was informed that the "pro boxer" on the receiving end of my left hook had filed a complaint with the police department, alleging that the force of my punch caused him to suffer "double vision." When word of this complaint reached the police ranks, that single encounter apparently bestowed a reputation. Bosses saw I could handle walking the toughest streets with SFPD's regulars, increasing the frequency of my assignments in the most violent sectors of the Fillmore. Fifty-one years later, a gathering of retired policemen were discussing old-time San Francisco policing at Westlake Joe's in Daly City when one of the officers recounted the story of the punch that resounded into the ages. Auld Lang Syne.

John Minderman has returned to San Francisco and has assumed the title of Chaplain for the San Francisco Veteran Police Officer's Association. After serving as a San Francisco Police Officer for a number of years John resigned and entered the Federal Bureau of Investigation from which he recently retired. Pictured above in the 1960's is Edward H. Hartman, John, and Solo Motorcycle Officer Ed McMills.

8

MIDNIGHT WATCH

The Traveler

One fateful Christmas morning, I encountered one of the most threatening incidents in my years as a police officer. It began with a routine start at midnight, falling in and receiving orders from the lieutenant. I'd recently been transferred from Northern Station to The Mission, and my partner that midnight watch was Dennis, a good-looking, experienced, intelligent officer, who seemed to possess great potential. Denny, as he was known, was the "designated operator" of the Mission 2 car, meaning he was the driver and decision-maker, and I was the helper.

We started patrol by traveling west on 18th Street toward Twin Peaks, into the heart of the Castro. At the corner of Sanchez, we parked the car, and I followed Denny into a bar. Denny appeared to know the bartender as he confidently ordered a "Traveler"—this turned out to be bourbon and a splash of water in a twelve-ounce Coke bottle with a liquor-bottle cork plug in the top. This passed as a portable container, fitting nicely in one of the inside pockets of a cloth patrol jacket or tucked into a cloth bag resting on the seat of a patrol car. As our watch proceeded and hours rolled along, Denny would occasionally take a nip from the Traveler.

There was a series of routine calls, nothing exciting. While Santa soared through the heavens in his sleigh, it seemed that nobody but he and the police were awake. It was the quietest morning I'd ever experienced. Denny and I were on call at the station killing time around 6:20 a.m., when a radio blared, "Attention, all units." An all-channel-broadcast meant something urgent was happening. It was a "211"—an armed robbery in progress at the Travelodge on Valencia at Market. We ran to the rear parking lot, jumped into our radio car, powered up, and wheeled around a couple of corners, driving as fast as possible toward Market Street some thirteen blocks away. The siren was off, in stealth mode, but red lights illuminated our urgent path.

Denny passed me the key to the shotgun, which was racked vertically and locked between us against the dashboard. I protested, "Come on, Denny, it'll be over by the time we get there."

Annoyed and adamant, Denny ordered me: "Take the damn gun out, John." Denny was the operator; he was in charge, so I had no choice. Reluctantly I complied, inserted the key into the lock, and took out the shotgun.

We arrived at the Travelodge, semi-alert and fighting fatigue seven hours into our shift. Exiting our car, we briefly scoped out the scene, then cautiously headed to the motel's front office. Per Denny's instructions, I carried with me the semi-automatic Remington "riot" shotgun with its 18-inch barrel. It was loaded with several rounds, each one packed with multiple shot about the individual size of .32-caliber bullets. Each fired round exited the barrel at several hundred feet per second faster than our .38-caliber pistol bullets. Even with today's modern weapons, police still keep that fearsome, formidable "blaster" available.

The visibly shaken motel clerk nervously informed us that the armed robber had fled about five minutes before we arrived. By now he could be long gone. Denny questioned the motel clerk as I stood by, feeling restless, with the shotgun butt resting against my hip. "What kind of gun did he have?" It soon became apparent that the clerk didn't know the difference between a semi-automatic and a revolver. Denny removed his six shot, 4-inch revolver and showed it to the clerk, asking, "Did it look like this?"

"It sure did, but it was much bigger." We concluded the robber wielded an unusually large .45-caliber, 6-inch revolver, which was one destructive handgun. As Denny continued with the clerk, I decided to look like I was doing something (image is everything), so I went out to make a search of the parking lot. It was a real long shot, but maybe the robber didn't flee the scene at all and was still lurking about.

In the lot, there were three cars parked parallel to each other, facing a brick wall. I approached and checked underneath each car and saw nothing. I looked down the length of each car to see if anyone was hiding, crouched down, between the cars and the wall. Seeing nothing, I continued walking and checked out the rest of the expansive parking lot, empty but for a police patrol wagon circling in the distance. I decided to return to check on Denny and the motel clerk. As I walked by the rear of the three parked cars a second time, I thought, "Why not take another look?" Leaning in from the back of each car to gain a better view of the space between the front fender and the wall, I checked the first car. Nothing. The second car. Nothing.

Approaching the final car, I stood on tiptoes to gain an extra inch and a half on my 6'4" height. This just barely brought into view the top of a man's head. My heart raced and mouth went dry. I leveled the shotgun downward, ordering, "Put your hands up and stand up...

slowly." Two hands shot up as a small man rose to his feet, pleading in an exhorting voice, "Don't shoot! Don't shoot!"

We went back and forth, individually echoing each other's orders: "Don't move!" "Don't move!" I needed backup right away. I couldn't see his gun, or know where it was. Maybe he threw it away, as robbers sometimes do; maybe not. What to do? I couldn't put the shotgun down to cuff him, not knowing where his gun was, so I put the stock of the heavy shotgun under my right arm and pressed it against my hip. I had my finger on the trigger as I reached with my left hand for the whistle on my belt. The shrill whistle got the attention of Denny, whom I was relieved to see running into the parking lot, long seconds later.

The two of us took the robber into custody. Our search revealed that his fully loaded .45-caliber revolver was in his right cowboy boot, and he had an additional twenty-two rounds tucked into his front pants pocket. We escorted the cuffed robber into the office, where the clerk identified him. As we interviewed "Mr. Hold-Up," he said he lived across the street. We wondered why he'd not just run home, where he'd probably never have been found. That run, however, would've required crossing the extended width of highly visible Market Street.

He told us he was a former US Marine and was a "walk-away" from the VA psychiatric hospital in Palo Alto. The Marines teach recruits "cover and concealment," so he exercised this technique, planning to eventually surface when everyone (Denny and me) left the scene. We took the robber to the back of the summoned patrol wagon. As he mounted the first step, I asked him, "I walked right by you, stood with my back to you. Why didn't you shoot me?" The highly trained Marine vet replied, "Things might've been different if you weren't carrying the shotgun." Thanks, Denny.

Club Unique

Distinctive black tiles formed a perfect background for big, neon-illuminated, white scroll letters proclaiming *Club Unique,* owned by a nasty man who catered to an edgy blue-collar crowd ready to spend money. One night, an elusive offender "ditched" several cops who were in foot pursuit. A cop who drank in the place tipped us that the owner hid the fleeing suspect above a false ceiling in the bar to help him evade arrest. We were definitely not happy, and a few days later, *Club Unique* would experience payback.

Lt. Ken Himmelstoss assembled us in a room to announce our response: "Every morning at 1:40 a.m., take the Paddy Wagon and the '1' car out of service and double-park them outside the Club Unique with your 'reds' on. Anybody coming out of the club who has 'a little heat on,' throw 'em in the wagon and book 'em 152."

Section 152 of the Municipal Police Code made it an offense to be drunk in public. How drunk was "drunk enough" to qualify for a ride and booking? It was at the officer's discretion.

For the next two weeks, we stood by in the early morning hours outside the club. At wit's end, the owner soon called the captain, who told him, "It's Lieutenant Himmelstoss's call to make."

We all witnessed the barkeep begging for reprieve within the lieutenant's glass-walled office. *Club Unique* survived, with an attitude adjustment, and in the future they'd think twice before messing with Mission cops.

Who's Got Your Back

Just after the first of the year in 1962, Lt. Ken Himmelstoss called Officer Charles J. Anderson, Star #424, and me into his "fishbowl" glass cubicle watch commander's office. Joe Brodnick, the regular operator of the Mission 1 car, had been placed on sick leave, with a massive attack of stomach ulcers. He would be off at least six weeks, then on "light duty" status indefinitely. No heavy patrolling in his future.

The Captain had decided to beef up our radio car presence by employing "the first" two-man car in The Mission. Would Charley and I like to be that team? Although we were in the same Academy class (the 87th), our interaction had been limited but pleasant. We momentarily glanced at one another and individually replied, "Why, sure" and "Yeah." Thus began a three-year partnership, which yielded dozens of felony arrests, meritorious awards, and over thirty commendations.

At five feet eleven inches tall, with a wiry build, pale Nordic complexion, and thinning blond hair, Charley appeared deceptively "average." His consistent, quiet, but engaging manner and well-spoken voice quickly identified him as at least one step ahead of the pack, more likely two or three. He walked casually and carried himself unthreateningly, but confidently, ever alert and quick to figure out a situation. Charley adroitly interspersed humor with probing dialogue, often eliciting incriminating statements from suspects without them realizing what had happened. We never spoke about ambitions and goals: our focus became and remained opportunistic, quality police work. Many hours on duty were spent either handling "runs" (radio-dispatched assignments), or on calculated, directed "patrollin'" with an eye toward "on view," or intercepting, spotting, and engaging "the bad guys" before or after a crime escapade.

Charley graduated from Mission High School and grew up close to where I was born and raised in the heart of the Mission District. We knew it from the inside out, but from different perspectives. Charley was a journeyman sheet metal worker, and I was the college graduate eight years his junior. We balanced one another nicely: I was socially reserved and somewhat emotionally cautious and distant, while Charley was polite but outgoing and engaging. We had a very easy way of working together. When a "situation" occurred, whoever had the right tools in his skill set stepped forward, the other partner playing sidekick. I always knew Charley had my back, a real necessity in our line of work.

His "intuitive compass—balancing reason and instinct," [Francis P. Cholle—*The Intuitive Compass*] rarely failed us, and frequently put us in the middle of where a good cop always wants to be—preventing a crime or catching the perpetrators. He had a knack for figuring out where crooks would be "holed-up," and possessed unbelievable, quietly engaging, confidence-building interviewing capabilities. We obtained confessions and admissions by the boatload because of his insightful, phenomenal core ability to "read people."

Charley's sense of humor defused many tense moments. One afternoon, directly in front of our black-and-white, a middle-aged woman blew through a red light at a major intersection, nearly triggering a multicar collision. All cars stopped as everyone watched for our reaction. Charley alighted from the police car in dramatic form and purposefully walked up to the chagrined, shaken violator. He delivered a brief, finger-waving lecture, whereupon she extended her hand tentatively outside her open driver's window. Charley lightly grasped her hand and administrated a very public, gentle "slap on the wrist" rebuke. Everybody cracked up. Case closed.

Off the Wagon

Early one Saturday morning, my partner Charley and I were dispatched to a "fight in progress" call at a bar called *Frankie and Johnny's* on 18th Street in The Castro. Bartenders rarely called police for assistance, since "documented incidents" might reflect poorly for the half-dozen licenses they needed to operate.

As we strode cautiously through the double doors, we saw the place was packed. Cigarette smoke partly obscured jostling bodies and flying fists some twenty feet ahead. Time for "hats and bats." Hats pulled tight, pocket clubs in hand, we aggressively yet unprovocatively pushed forward through the thrusting, alcohol-fueled crowd into the large, deep room. "Police. Move aside. Make way."

Yells and profanities filled the air. We absorbed some pushes and sideways glancing blows from the milling crowd, and answered with correspondingly harder strikes. Control would come at the end of our clubs. Most people moved as we edged purposefully toward the group of fighting patrons. Reaching them, we struck quick, stabbing body blows to the engaged opponents, who sagged against the bar or faded from the fight.

An attractive, drunken, aggressive woman had apparently triggered the initial difficulty that evolved into a brawl. The fighting had stopped, and threatening men hovered around us as we cuffed up the mouthy woman. She resisted restraint, encouraging the men to rescue her. We struggled to keep her under control and found our path to the exit ahead blocked. I looked at the biggest, scowling blocker. Brandishing my club, I said, "One way or another, we're going out of here!" Firmly grasping the prisoner, we hunched over, clubs ready, bodies set, moving resolutely forward over the forty-five feet toward the door.

Curses and threats came our way as I repeatedly, but cautiously, shoved and pushed, ordering, "Out of my way!" No soft-shoe policing here. We hit the front door and burst onto the sidewalk, the drunken mob trailing, a bit back on their heels, but still determined to interfere. Patrons spilled onto the sidewalk and street. With the woman handcuffed behind her back, I lifted her over a handy parking meter and set her down, so she couldn't escape. She requested a restroom break, which I declined. What followed wasn't pretty.

Just then, the Paddy Wagon appeared along with another radio car. Even with the extra backup, it took some effort to defuse the atmosphere by tossing additional aggressors into the wagon—order restored. Edgy policing with narrow margins and menace had a certain appeal— defining one's personal and professional worth. It's what separated you from ordinary citizenry, meeting and overcoming bedrock challenges of preserving a peaceful society.

Hide the Bottle

Cops and firefighters play crucial roles in public safety, and their responsibilities overlap, often bringing them together. Their roles also differ in distinct ways. This obscure melding sometimes begets confusing rivalry, not always friendly. Fighting fires is dangerous and potentially lethal, yet many calls for firefighters have nothing to do with fires: medical emergencies, tending to people after automobile crashes, even rescuing kittens from treetops—all tasks the public appreciates, as opposed to arresting people and carting them to jail. In the 1960s, dozens of San Francisco police officers transferred to the fire department, which seemed to generally offer a much more comfortable lifestyle. Flexible time schedules allowed them to work two days on and three days off, and many "full-time" firemen could juggle another career or educational pursuit, like studying law. All this while getting to cavort around in big, manly red trucks wearing futuristic superhero uniforms.

One foggy midnight shift, at 3:10 a.m., Charley and I were dispatched in the Mission 1 car to 24th and Bryant Street, where we were to assist with traffic and crowd control because of a fire in a bar. On scene we saw no need for either traffic or crowd control at this wee hour. Our role was to just maintain a presence while the fire units battled to contain a fairly serious fire. The brave men brought the smoky fire under control. With the smoke dissipating, the firemen grabbed heavy canvas tarps and entered the bar. We wondered, could there be bodies inside the bar to be carried out?

As the firemen came out of the bar, we saw that it took one man at either end, with a big, sagging hump in the middle, to carry each of the heavy tarps. These weren't bodies. It must be burnt debris from the fire scene. Most of the big, sagging humps were dumped at the curb. However, some were carried with extreme care to the fire truck, lifted ever so gently in, and snugly deposited by hand just behind the cab. What could it be?

"Aha." Our simmering detective juices kicked in. This was not debris; it was booze. Some firemen were occasionally known to like a drink, just like the cops. The pack of police officers waited for their chance to pounce, like coyotes. Timing was crucial. "Timing matters—Timing is everything. Whether you are making high-stakes business decisions or personal choices, you must decide not only what to do, but when to do it. Act too early or too late, and the results can be disappointing...even disastrous." [Stuart Albert: *When: The Art of Perfect Timing*]

After several loads, the firemen went back into the bar for their probable last load, and the coyote pack struck. Moments later, the firemen left the bar for the final time. They smiled in our direction as they mounted the truck with their last load of pirate's booty and peered into the section in the back of the cab. Finding it empty, shocked, angry expressions grew on their faces as they turned their glaring eyes toward the coyotes.

Doubled Over

The dreaded double-back shift prompted one close call for me. Charley and I caught a '418': a family fight, at about 10:25 p.m. on Shotwell Street. Exhausted, dispirited, and distracted in the midst of a double-back shift, we entered a dark, old Victorian house, which was segmented into individual apartments.

Ascending a long flight of stairs, we found a couple with an infant child. The lighting was dim, and we weren't paying enough attention to pick up on cues. The woman holding her baby wasn't very communicative and kept throwing the man fearful looks and glances. Perhaps separation with privacy would spur communication. I brought the woman and baby into their apartment to converse. She was just starting to exhibit trust when I heard a loud shout, followed by a series of crashes. I exited to the landing, my eyes sweeping down the stairs, where I saw Charley in a heap and the male aggressor halfway down, apparently en route to finish him off.

Club in hand, I yelled a profane challenge at the assailant, who stopped, reversed, and charged toward me. Mission accomplished. Set and ready, I swung a hard blow at his shoulders and neck. It struck off aim and he fell to one knee, blood spewing forth. Down, but not out. A hard kick to the body, and he doubled over. I cuffed up our fighter and tended to my fallen partner, who fortunately soon recovered from the vicious blow that had sent him hurtling. We discovered our arrestee had a substantial drug stash in the apartment and was afraid that the woman was going to tip us. Drugs weren't even on our radar before—but they were now.

Four Roses

On a 4:00 p.m.-to-midnight shift, I was alone in the Mission Station 1 car. It was rare that I didn't have my regular partner, Charley, with me, and I was feeling slightly vulnerable. A radio call interrupted: "Proceed to the station and see the lieutenant." This man wasn't our regular lieutenant, but a fill-in very familiar with the district. The man had a ruddy face and wore his white dress shirt with gold collar bars quite proudly.

Lieutenants, known as watch commanders, were in charge of the district in the absence of the captain. Many of these men were known as the real commanders of the district, much more forceful leaders than captains, who often seemed detached and remote. The lieutenant at Mission Station literally sat on high, on an elevated rostrum in the middle of all the activity. His glass cubicle was a fishbowl, with windows on all sides so as watch commander he could literally watch everything that went on.

In my experience, most lieutenants were seasoned, hard, effective leaders. They took no guff from anybody, least of all the policemen who worked for them. They varied in temperament and personality, but most were wise and possessed excellent judgment and resolve. Many were extremely practical, having passed examinations and survived decades of shift work, departmental politics, and gritty street experience.

This particular lieutenant was a bit of an exception. His complexion and chubby fullness reflected his proclivity to drink slightly more than average. Any time an officer received a call to return to the station and see the lieutenant, he felt some dread. A lieutenant never called you just to pass the time of day or give you a compliment. It was always a difficulty, usually serious. As I walked into the lieutenant's glass cubicle, he called out, "Mindermann, you got the '1' car?" I answered in the affirmative.

The lieutenant continued, "Go up to The Expansion Bar and pick up a case. They've got a case for us." I figured this was not a case for investigation; this was a case for consumption. It was just before Christmas—'tis the season for bottles to be dispensed. A lot of liquor flowed into the hands of San Francisco police around Christmastime: gifts and thank-yous from merchants all over the district. It was a big San Francisco tradition. However, not everybody shared in the booty equally. I left the station a bit annoyed, as I didn't feel comfortable walking into The Expansion, picking up a case of liquor, and transporting it in the police car back to the station.

The Expansion was a huge bar on Market Street near 14th frequented by seamen and workingmen of every type. It was unusual for a bar to have two entrances—one on Market Street and the other on 14th, providing covert access and egress options. Slightly irritated, I double-parked the radio car, partially blocking Market Street, and put on all the emergency and warning lights. In full uniform, I walked into the bar and told the bartender that the lieutenant sent me for "the case." He promptly picked up and handed over a heavy twelve-bottle case of Four Roses bourbon. I carried it out of the bar to Market Street, and into the trunk went Mr. Booze, currency of the season. What great use of my time and skills.

Back at Mission Station, I carried the bourbon into an absent lieutenant's office. I stashed it underneath his desk, out of sight, as there was always the possibility of other officers availing themselves of a bottle. I scurried out of the station, back into my car and onto the street, feeling relieved to be back in service.

I hadn't gone two blocks when a call came over the radio in ominous tones: "Mission 1, 902 the station. See the lieutenant immediately."

I thought to myself, "Uh-oh, something's really wrong. What happened? A bottle or two missing? I'm in deep trouble."

Back in the station, I hurried into the lieutenant's office. He was obviously angry, his face a heated, fiery red. Barely able to contain himself, he pointed his finger at the offending case of Four Roses, demanding, "Did you bring in this sh*t?"

"Yes, sir," I replied.

The lieutenant looked at me hard and in his finest leadership voice gave me an order. "You take this back and tell them we don't drink this sh*t."

Shocked, I cautiously asked the lieutenant, "You want me to tell him...in those exact words?"

Came the reply, "Absolutely. You tell them exactly what I said."

"Yes, sir." Once again I proceeded to The Expansion, double-parked on Market Street, threw on all the reds and cautions, unloaded the bourbon, slammed the trunk, and marched inside. All eyes fell on me and the case of bourbon, as it must have been a once-in-a-lifetime experience for a cop to be seen carrying liquor *into* a tavern. I walked to the end of the bar, the bartender following me, looking concerned and confused.

I heaved the case of booze on top of the bar with a thump and stared directly at the bartender, saying, "Look, these are the words of the lieutenant. I'm only the messenger boy here. He told me to tell you that we don't drink this sh*t."

The bartender was incredulous. "He really said that?"

"That's exactly what he said."

He asked, "Well, what does he want?"

"Could you give me something a little better?" Musing a bit, he said, "Well how about Early Times?"

I inquired, "Is that better?" and he assured me, "It's...a little better."

"OK, let's try that." Taking the Early Times, I returned to Mission Station and deposited the booze at the lieutenant's feet. A little smile crinkled over his face as he relaxed and nodded that I'd performed

OK. When initially instructing me, the lieutenant employed the collaborative "we" and "us" (as in "*We* don't drink this sh*t," and "He's got a case for *us.*"). Alas, "we" and "us" did not carry over into the transaction's distribution phase, as the twelve bottles eventually found their way into final hands, mine not included.

Tips from the Bottom

Early in my police career, I was contacted by SFPD Captain Francis (Frank) Harrington, head Police Academy trainer. He noted my teaching background and accomplishments in patrol activities, and as there was no block of instruction within the current curriculum in basic recruit training for "How to Patrol," he asked if I would be willing to develop and teach a two-hour course in that area.

Frank was a handsome, tall Irishman with sharp, angular features and a full head of coal-black hair. My dad worked under Frank (a lieutenant at the time) on the Taxicab Detail. During my formative years, all SF Police were required to live in The City, so cops socialized together. Today's suburban dispersal of officers in the vast Bay Area hinterland changed those dynamics.

Frank Harrington's professional relationship with my Dad evolved, as did many, into an inter-family relationship with his wife and kids. Frank had come to San Francisco from Montana, seeking opportunity as a young man in the mid-1930s, during the grinding, seemingly entrenched poverty of the Great Depression. His father was an Irish immigrant who worked as a miner.

Frank was a quiet, reserved, smart guy. Having passed a highly competitive police examination, he'd found himself initially assigned to walking around the World's Fair for a couple of years at Treasure Island (TI)—in the middle of San Francisco Bay—in the late '30s. I gathered that his initial TI assignment was not bad for a young officer, who came into daily contact with the dancers, water follies performers, and other female entertainers while he "made his rounds." Not all policing is gritty, dangerous, and "at the sharp end."

I jumped at the chance to create a "How to Patrol" course and distributed a survey instrument to a number of officers who I knew were highly proficient "go-getters," seeking their insights about effective, productive patrol strategy, tactics, and methods. They were helpful and almost seemed honored to be thus solicited. Based on the their observations, and drawing on my own personal experiences, I authored a two-hour lecture entitled "Tips from the Bottom," as the patrol assignment was the entry-level job in the police department.

The audience for my course would be a roomful of easily bored recruits, who were enduring weeks of dull instruction about proper report writing and arcane rules and regulations. I embellished the curriculum with vivid incidents and stories to pique their interest, a practice that laid the foundation for the teaching approach I would later develop at the FBI National Academy at Quantico.

Sticky Fingers

At 3:30 a.m. a burglar alarm activated at the Haslett warehouse, located close by, but within the Southern Police District. Our help was needed to search this large, multi-storied structure containing a virtual gold mine of diversified, valuable items. A half dozen of us, supplemented by a search dog & police handler, went floor to floor, finding no indication of actual forced entry or burglary. Perhaps wind or the vibrations emanating from speeding big-rigs on a nearby freeway had set off the alarm. False alarms were the norm.

When we completed our search and exited, we were surprised to see a uniformed Southern District Sergeant standing outside within the vicinity of our police cars. The dog handling police officer approached the rear of his police station wagon and instantly sounded off in a loud, accusatory voice, "whoever put this sh*t in here better get it out!" All of us zeroed in on the rear of his wagon where several new appearing rifles and shotguns rested just inside the open tailgate.

Needing no further prompting, the Sergeant spoke up, directly addressing the Dog Officer "Walt, meet me in the alley alongside Southern Station." I personally knew Walt from my rookie tour at Northern Station. He had been the Operator of the 2-car which handled the toughest area of a difficult police district. He was an honest, effective, hard-working Officer who had volunteered to take on the additional responsibilities of being a dog handler. He was also very direct and forthright. His intently staring eyes bored in on the suspect Sergeant; "did you put these guns in my wagon?"

The Sergeant retorted in an edgy, commanding voice, "I told you to meet me alongside Southern Station." It appeared that our burglarizing Sergeant's plan was to transfer the filched guns from Walt's wagon to his personal car positioned in an alley alongside Southern Station. One of the uncomfortable rumors circulating concerned a "burglary gang" of Southern police officers.

Walt's gaze momentarily looked away from the Sergeant but came back, locking on hard, not backing down, voicing an ultimatum: "Look, whoever put those guns in my wagon better get them out now or I'm going to Southern Station and book them into evidence as found property." That action would have placed the stolen guns into an official channel, which would have insured eventual accountability and identification of the Sergeant as a thief. Frustrated and agitated, the Sergeant struggled as he picked up the guns and began toting them back inside the warehouse. We stood stunned as this standoff drama played out. Son of a gun.

A few years later, my Dad, a retired police sergeant, was happily employed as a security officer on the evening shift of the downtown Hilton

Hotel. Dad announced that the "stealing sergeant" (now retired) had
been hired in a security capacity by the Hilton. I warned my Dad:
"Don't do it, that guy is a thief. You'll have nothing but problems with
him." My Dad seemed surprised and disappointed that I would accuse
the new hired hand of thievery. Soon after, hotel guests noticed personal
items missing from their rooms.

Fired Up

Close to 4:00 a.m., Charlie and I were relaxing, enjoying a cup of coffee at Mel's Drive-In on 140 South Van Ness Avenue, a classic post–
WWII semicircle, modernistic, almost art-deco structure. On the
outdoor speakers, Rusty Draper sang a kind of gospel blues version of
his hit "Night Life," which went, "Night life ain't the good life, but
it's my life." It kind of fit us. Suddenly our police radio blared forth:
"Attention all units—a working '528' at the Hotel Sherman—11th
and Mission." "Working" meant: *actual flames sighted on a reported fire.*
The hotel housed dozens of older, single people; had been built after the
1906 earthquake, with all wood construction; and consisted of three
floors above ground-level businesses. Its location was a quick block and
a half away.

Down Mission Street we shot with an immediate view of the entire upper floor fully enveloped in flames. Our car came to a juddering
stop with audible sirens in the distance. Firemen were on the way, but
not yet there. I jumped up, grasping the lower steel rung of the pull-
down, access ladder to the fire escape. Down it noisily clanked, and up
I scrambled. A look through the access window down the first floor
hallway showed residents scrambling about with no immediate hazard.

Up the fire escape I continued. The second floor hallway was a bit
hazy, with thickening smoke and flames peeking through the ceiling. In I went, feeling instant warmth as I ran door to door knocking,

kicking, and yelling, "Fire—get out!" Any unopened door I kicked in. Residents were perplexed and confused. I ordered them to the 11th Street stairs. One occupant said he had to find his hat before leaving. I upstaged his hat search, grabbing his arm and pulling him into the hallway, saying, "Out—NOW!"

The heat and smoke grew intense—varying shades of blue, orange, red, and yellow flames, like gas jets, shot and whooshed along the hallway ceiling. A big fireman struggled to pull a heavy, charged hose line down the hallway from 11th Street, preparing to "crack the valve" and shoot a blast of water. About twenty-five feet distant, we momentarily faced off. The ceiling then heaved, making a horrible, deep rumbling sound, as it actually undulated. We were instantly frozen in place.

The fireman dropped the hose, turned around, and ran for the 11th Street stairwell—he knew more than me, so I followed suit, turning and sprinting for the Mission Street fire escape, as small embers began raining down on my hat and epilates. I descended as quickly as possible and made it safely to the sidewalk. Fortunately nobody died because our Mission 1 car was in the right place at the right time. That early morning cup of Mel's coffee we'd needed may have saved lives.

9

CUT TO THE CHASE

On a midnight watch approaching 2:25 a.m., Charley and I rolled out the back of Mission Station in our squad car onto San Jose Avenue. Early morning fog hung overhead, blanketing the quiet city. Rather than take my normal right turn toward our patrol area, boredom compelled me to turn left. A subsequent right onto 24th Street brought us abruptly to a hilly neighborhood with undersized lanes, narrow, twisting alleys, and sidewalks so steep they were engraved with concrete stairs. Our car glided to a halt at a stop sign on a flat section of 24th Street at streetcar-tracked Church Street. I noticed an MG sports car approaching from the west, followed tightly by a pickup truck—the two vehicles so close they appeared to be in tandem. Both slowly came to a full halt at the opposite stop sign.

In recent weeks we'd lost lots of cars to auto thieves in Twin Peaks. The sports car seemed a likely theft candidate and the closely trailing truck a probable support vehicle. We sat across the intersection from one another locked in a distant stare-down. Tension took hold. Who would blink? I turned to Charley. "Let's see where they go." The MG took a sharp left directly across our path, accelerating north on Church, followed quickly by the pickup. I hung a hard right directly behind the truck. Both suspicious vehicles accelerated and made a wide left turn at midblock into Elizabeth Alley, barely nineteen feet wide.

It was on. "Hit the lights and siren." The MG and truck funneled up the alley and we fell in behind, front red light illuminated, siren blaring, engine growling, and police radio turned up to the max. All three vehicles gyrated up the constricted alley. The siren echoed harshly off the close building walls. As we picked up speed, my partner began calling out the chase for police communications. Rapidly approaching the intersection of Sanchez, neither vehicle showed any sign of slowing. Suddenly the sports car braked sharply and took a screeching left onto Sanchez, while the truck hung a right to go north. Which one to pursue? Over the siren, I yelled at my partner, "Let's take the MG!"

He answered, "Let's go!"

Heading south on Sanchez, the MG took a quick left and doubled back on 24th Street. A three-block straightaway encouraged the MG driver to accelerate to sixty miles an hour, until he abruptly braked before hitting an awkward right turn at Dolores. Trailing, I took this turn with my car in the oncoming lane, braking hard with my heel, still pressing the gas pedal with my toes, revving the engine. With an inferior car, this gave us maximum power when I released the brake, and helped us keep up with faster cars. (In over a dozen all-out street chases, only one driver in a stolen Pontiac Grand Prix ever out-powered us, by smartly taking the long 17th Street hill toward Twin Peaks.)

Our engine at full throttle whined, high-pitched, over the wailing siren. The assault on our senses—by all the noise, speed, and maneuvering—fueled the exhilaration of the chase. I slammed the car hard through the turn onto Dolores Street, a wide thoroughfare bisected by large center islands with grass and palm trees. Here and there the center islands break to allow traffic to pass from one side of the street to the other. Cresting Dolores Street (a steep hill) at Jersey Street, listening to the engine strain, I caught a startling glimpse of the MG, which abruptly swerved and cut across the broad boulevard, driving at dangerously high speeds, on the wrong side of the street, directly into oncoming traffic. Instinctively locked in a zone, I mirrored the MG maneuver.

Both of us were now on the wrong side of southbound Dolores, approaching a steep drop-off—a blind horizon. The MG took a hard left east at 25th Street and disappeared over one of the city's steepest drop-offs. Suddenly a De Soto taxicab came into view, speeding at me head on. He deftly pulled to his right, and we passed "eyeball to eyeball." His expression: "I don't believe this."

Continuing pursuit, I quickly turned left, plunging down 25th Street, a block so steep the sidewalks had stairs. My front wheels momentarily lost contact with the ground before landing with a crash and shimmy as we barreled down after the MG. Ahead of us, the MG leaned a harsh left onto Fair Oaks and accelerated up the narrow street. We crested a rise at midblock and took a right on to 24th Street. Suddenly, the MG was facing another police car head on. The sports car skidded to an abrupt stop, boxed in between the two prowl cars.

The MG driver attempted to reverse, but only succeeded in grinding his gears. Quickly alighting, he evasively attempted to run east, to no avail. He was in custody. The MG wasn't the only stolen vehicle. Charley and I canvassed the Noe Valley neighborhood and located the truck that had been following the MG. It was parked in front of an address on Elizabeth Street, very close to the starting point of the chase. A radio check of the plates revealed the registrant made three mistakes: (1) Illegally switching license plates; (2) Parking the truck in front of his own address; (3) Being at home when we came to call.

The truck itself was also stolen. We searched, or "tossed," his residence (incidental to arrest) and found a criminal mother lode—a set of lock picks, three rings of about a dozen vehicle ignition keys each, seven capsules of Methedrine, and a photocopied Selective Service card.

The sum total of the adventure was two stolen vehicles, fraudulent use of vehicle license plates, burglary tools, three sets of master auto ignition keys, a drug stash, and illegally reproduced federal documents recovered. This dynamic duo was an entrepreneurial criminal enterprise and auto-theft ring unto themselves, and when we intercepted them they were en route to dump off the freshly stolen MG in a wrecking yard south of Market, bordering the Mission, a possible staging area and disposal site. The arrests resulting from my unplanned, boredom-induced left turn substantially cut down auto thieving in Twin Peaks.

Baby-Blue Cadillac

One midnight shift I was assigned to ride with Jerry McNaughton, operator of the Mission 2 car, as we policed Noe Valley and Twin Peaks. Jerry embodied the balanced, intelligent model of a community-oriented police officer—he consistently offered distressed citizens excellent counseling and guidance, yet wasn't hesitant in bringing the full force of the law upon criminals, thugs, and predators. His quality policing and insightful, humane judgment caught the eye of the Chief, who brought him on his executive staff as a Sergeant.

At 12:25 a.m. a call came over the radio indicating a pursuit in progress of a large, baby-blue Cadillac convertible in an adjacent district, the Ingleside. Unfortunately, this midnight shift we'd been assigned something known as a "relief car." It gave anything but relief. It was a stand-in car, on the verge of being junked, that we used when our regular vehicle was being serviced. This one had a hole in the floorboards near the brake and clutch pedals, and a severe case of the shakes and shimmies. It jumped, vibrated, shook, sputtered, hesitated, and groaned. As the pursuit approached our vicinity, Jerry turned to me, asking, "You think we can help?"

"Sure," I replied.

"What can we do?" queried Jerry.

I replied, "I don't know, but let's go down 24ᵗʰ Street and sit near Guerrero. That's where it's headed." We sat on 24ᵗʰ, engine idling, prepared to join the pursuit, hearing the high-pitched, oscillating siren getting louder as the radio broadcast from the pursuing police car called out the play-by-play. Very shortly the baby-blue Cadillac, with its headlights off, whizzed by northbound on Guerrero Street. We barely got a glimpse as it cleared 24ᵗʰ at over sixty miles per hour.

In the distance we heard an almost pitiful squeal, the thin, wailing siren of the Ingleside Unit. Ten seconds later a gallant but underpowered police car came charging through the intersection, red lights blazing, as the distance widened between it and the Cadillac convertible.

Jerry asked, "What do you think we should do?"

"Well, let's sit here; maybe it'll come back," I replied, knowing full well we had no chance of catching anything in our dilapidated pile of junk. Even new, our squad cars were no match for a Cadillac. The Caddy was Detroit's premier American muscle, while our squad cars were Detroit's lowest-end, six-cylinder, standard sedans, not geared for much more than cruising around, and certainly not for aggressive pursuits.

We lay in wait, listening as the radio choreographed the chase, which by then was winding around some twelve blocks distant. Soon, though, the hunt returned to Guerrero Street, coming again in our direction. A radio voice counted out the numbered streets of the pursuing Ingleside unit, "16ᵗʰ...17ᵗʰ...18ᵗʰ...19ᵗʰ...20ᵗʰ...21ˢᵗ..."

"Jerry, they'll be here," I said in a rising voice. Swish! The blue Caddy flew by at seventy miles per hour southbound in the opposite direction. Falling farther behind, the beleaguered, gutsy Ingleside unit came through the intersection about twenty seconds later, accompanied by the beaten voice of an Ingleside cop notifying communications, "We lost the Caddy."

Jerry turned to me, "What should we do?"

Given our vehicular limitations, it was hard to know what "proper police action" demanded, but I never hesitated about playing a hunch. I answered, "Let's take a ride up Noe Valley. Maybe something will happen." We reversed and headed back up 24th Street, then meandered south to 25th. We were westbound on 25th when suddenly the baby-blue Caddy whizzed by, lights out, one hundred feet directly in front of us, heading north on Sanchez and blasting through intersections at outrageous speeds.

I grabbed the radio and contacted headquarters. "Mission 2, we've sighted the Cadillac and are going in pursuit." Excitement became palpable as once again the cops had hope—which is a big part of policing. Jerry floored it and we pursued the Cadillac for a couple of blocks, quickly losing sight of the powerful behemoth. "Mission 2, we lost 'em." Our spirits sank. In despair, we cruised the main business drag on 24th Street. Just west of Noe Street and short of Castro, the blue Caddy, lights still off, jack-rabbited, burning rubber out of a driveway fronting a commercial garage, and accelerated rapidly up 24th Street toward Twin Peaks. "Mission 2!" I yelled into the microphone. "We've got the Caddy again, west on 24th —in pursuit."

Radio dispatch shot back in elevated, enthusiastic tones: "All units, Mission 2 in pursuit of the Cadillac convertible, west of Noe, up 24th Street."

The Caddy took a hard left at Diamond, its first chance at a cross street. Jerry approached the intersection at high speed and prepared to turn left at Diamond, but he misjudged the distance, and we bounced erratically through a gas station, with Jerry veering around the gas pumps. Our clunker came to a skidding halt. Jerry slammed it into reverse, backing wildly to get back to the street. We resumed the chase back on 24th Street, then south on Diamond ascending a series of short blocks with increasingly steep grades. As we attempted to accelerate into each intersection, the front end smashed into pavement and our car bounced, shook, and groaned.

The Caddy had to be up there somewhere. Every once in a while, as we climbed ever higher, I thought I could see a bobbing, brake-lighted tail fin occasionally flashing like a lighthouse beacon. The eluder made a bad decision toward the top of Diamond Heights, taking a left on Army, going east down a ragged street obscured by shrubbery and abruptly ending in a warning barricade foreshadowing a steep drop to a rocky outcropping that awaited the unwary.

The convertible shot through the barricade with a boom, soaring briefly before crashing onto the rocks below. Disoriented, the young driver emerged from behind the wheel of the wreckage and scrambled out into our custody. Relief car—1; Caddy—0. "Mr. Speedster," it turned out, had appropriated the Cadillac from the garage on 24th Street, from which he jack-rabbited out in front of us in the final leg of the chase. His father owned that garage, and the kid, only about sixteen years old, was taking a customer's car on a joyride. Joyful it wasn't, but he was lucky to be alive.

The Speed Skater

The Tenderloin was an entrepreneurial criminal underworld, a career-building panorama for any cop who could capitalize on opportunity.

The area abounded with street predators of every stripe: muggers, purse-snatchers, thieves, drug- and stolen-property dealers, all stalking prey. And the cops saw the stalking criminals as their prey. At 10:30 p.m. one evening, I slowly meandered east on Golden Gate Avenue with my slouched-down partner Fred, who was taking law classes. We were in plain clothes, in an unmarked car.

About thirty of us aspiring (though mostly not-to-be) detectives were on the street to rove and engage criminal types in high-crime neighborhoods. This approach, dubbed Operation S ("Saturation"), seemed to prevent crime—keeping serial predators off balance by flooding a geographic zone, catching the criminals somewhat unawares, and hitting them with warrant checks and detailed "Interrogation Cards" (ICs). In precomputer police work, these three-by-five index cards helped track dates, times, and locations of certain people who were more likely to be involved in crime, containing identifying and descriptive information, with a brief justification for why the individual was targeted. Morning lineups of arrestees provided viewing detectives the opportunity to correlate ICs with documentation of suspects' criminal activities and known whereabouts.

Today many police departments use CompStat (Computer and Statistics) tracking and analysis systems—an approach conceived and implemented by William Bratton, former Los Angeles police chief and New York police commissioner. In *Collaborate or Perish,* Bratton and co-author Zachary Tumin emphasize: "In a world where everyone is connected, collaboration is the critical game changer, the difference maker, the force multiplier."

We approached the corner of Market Street and Taylor in the far-left of three lanes on a one-way street south of the Golden Gate Theatre. A young male appeared, crouched in classic speed-skater posture, scurrying up the sidewalk. Because there was no ice to be had, I guessed he was running, with both his hands firmly placed in the small of his back, leaning forward at almost a ninety-degree angle. "Fred, that guy's cuffed up!" I abruptly stopped our car, then quickly reversed past "the skater," stopping just short of Jones Street. I quickly hopped out, and into my arms came a wheezing escapee. Somewhere nearby, a police officer was surely looking for his missing handcuffs. Fred shook the skater down for weapons, then threw him into the back seat. "Lie down and don't move," he said.

Back behind the wheel, I said to Fred, "Let's have some fun with this." On this particularly dark block, we sat and listened intently to the police radio, knowing it would be a short wait until a desperate, disguised plea hit the airwaves. Cops have a "radio voice," usually commanding and in-control—except for the times when things are deteriorating and a little extra help is needed. With great anticipation, I awaited to savor the words and intonation from the officer who was missing handcuffs. (a.k.a. "Escaped Prisoner")

Bill Roberts was known simply as "The Voice" for his signature deep baritone. When riding with Bill (you never drove) in the Northern 1 car, he was always "The Operator," technically and quite seriously in command of the two-man crew. Most of us worked together without much fanfare about operator status. Not Bill. On my one ride with Bill, I sustained minor pain in my fingers when I reached for the microphone to answer a radio dispatch. The Voice slammed his right hand over my offending digits, saying, in his deep baritone, "When you ride with me, I handle all radio calls." The Voice desperately wanted to become a detective. Every time a new inspector appointment list came out, he was disappointed, selectively pointing to listed names, and droning, "That guy got it? Why, he couldn't find sand at the beach or apples in the orchard."

Bill was also noted for being superterritorial. Each car within a police district had a "sector," defined by street boundaries. We generally adhered to and respected sectors but moved freely around the overall district to handle calls and back up other cars. Bill once challenged another officer who happened to stray onto Bill's side of a boundary street. The transgressor got pretty hot, pointing to his star and saying to The Voice, "Read it—it says *San Francisco Police*, not Northern 1 or Northern 2."

At last, over the radio it came, a voice weak and plaintive. "Ahh… headquarters…could I have any available units '904' (meet me) in the 400 block of Taylor?"

The reply came, "What've you got, Central 2?"

"Ahh…nothing much…if you'll just have any S, Central, or Traffic unit…swing by for a minute, that's all."

Fred and I chuckled, exchanging knowing glances. Central 2 had lost his handcuffs. We slowly drove and turned left up Taylor. My destination would be that Central car, four blocks ahead. The skater had managed to run five blocks from his initial captors. Not too bad.

Taylor was the southern gateway to Nob Hill, each block increasingly steeper until that final ascent made it seem you were driving your way into heaven. Ahead, the street was alight with flashing yellows and reds. I crept up at ten miles per hour until I stopped at the outer ring of a convention of police cars and motorcycles with shuffling cops looking concerned.

A tall, midthirties Central officer ambled over, with a gravely concerned expression, as the situation deserved. As he scanned us, I casually asked, "You lose your cuffs?" Profanities spewed forth, as he sighted the skater lying across the rear seat. Our rear door was jerked open, and a herd of angry cops dragged the skater out. He was momentarily down on the street by our car. Fred and I moved out quickly. No sense hanging around this scene. We earned no thank-yous. That's policing.

The Dirty Ford

I was alone in a squad car one evening, working "Accident Investigation" in the far southeast section of The City—a vast landscape of abandoned shipbuilding, repair, and industrial facilities, interspersed with pockets of lower-middle-class residential neighborhoods. Public housing close to Hunters Point provided a constant stream of "beefs"—domestics, cuttings, stabbings, and shootings.

Working alone made you hyperaware of everything around you. Cars and people on foot continuously fed through your vision to be evaluated and filtered through your subconscious. On my way to an assignment involving a minor property-damage accident, I approached the intersection of Silver and San Bruno Avenues. I noticed a dirty-looking but newer-model Ford sedan cross in front of me, traveling east on Silver Avenue onto the Highway 101 overpass, occupied by two white males in their mid- to late twenties. Although there was nothing obviously wrong, instantly and instinctively I felt these guys did not fit the car and were up to no good. Author Francis P. Cholle, in *The Intuitive Compass,* describes this type of intuition as "the ability to know something directly, without analytic reasoning, bridging the gap between the conscious and unconscious parts of our mind, and also between instinct and reason."

The two guys in the Ford did a double take as they saw me. That fed my instinctive suspicion. Continuing on my assignment would've taken me south on San Bruno Avenue, but I diverted and swung a quick left turn, sliding in behind the dirty suspect vehicle. Immediately I noticed the license plate on the filthy car was surprisingly clean—the mismatch a sure sign the plate was stolen. "Reasonable suspicion" kicked in, saying something bigger was wrong. Cholle says, "Although sometimes difficult to understand, [intuition and instinct] very often point us in the right direction; sometimes they can even save our lives." I picked up the microphone and called in a priority: "Traffic 11, request-ing a rolling hot check, east on Silver, across the 101 Freeway from San Bruno, a 1966 Ford red sedan, occupied by two white males, California license…" Radio communications acknowledged, advising to stand by.

The passenger turned around, watching me. Through the Silver Terrace neighborhood we rolled, an isolated part of San Francisco with narrow streets and rolling, hilly terrain, filled with mostly single-fam-ily homes. The passenger continued turning around, eyeballing me. Tense seconds went by until a few blocks later, when the radio intoned, "Traffic 11, be advised that plate is reported stolen, and the subjects are '10-30' red." That broadcast meant that I not only had a probable stolen car with a stolen plate, but that the individuals occupying that car were two wanted felons tied to serious crimes.

I quickly barked back, "Traffic 11 requesting backup from any avail-able unit."

Communications acknowledged and put out an "all-channels" broadcast: *"Any available unit, Traffic 11 is following a '10-30' red ve-hicle east on Silver Avenue, from the 101 Freeway. Any unit to help."* Radio silence: nobody answering. I continued alone, following Mr. Dirty as the pleas from communications continued: *"Any available unit—to assist Traffic 11 with a 10-30 red vehicle."* Again, no response.

The criminals might at any time make a spontaneous, aggressive move. Act or react? There simply wasn't a correct answer, a single best or safest thing to do. The Dirty Ford moved east on Silver Avenue. I kept following the vehicle to buy time, letting them call the shots while hoping for help. I took my .41 Magnum from its holster, ready near my right hand, as I steered the car with my left. They weren't go-ing to get the jump on me. After a mile and a half with no help, we reached Third Street, a commercial strip in the Bayview. The Dirty Ford pulled into a Shell gas station and stopped.

Advising radio of my location, I stopped about thirty feet behind the dirty vehicle, opened my door, and took a kneeling firing position between the door and the body of the police car, aiming my pistol toward the subjects, who were opening the doors to their car. "Keep your hands up and visible, palms against the windshield where I can see them, and don't move." In that moment several Potrero police cars rolled into the station, and I was suddenly safer. I later learned these two felons were involved in a series of robberies and carjackings. Their base of operations was a bar in the Tenderloin called The Red Robin, which catered to a mixed bag of hoodlums and criminals.

The FBI and San Francisco police inspectors followed up my work with a collaborative investigation, resulting in another highly wanted felon being arrested in the Westlake area of Daly City. That last felon was an IO (Identification Order), a wanted fugitive subject of the FBI. (Years ago, these IOs were the basis of the FBI's "Ten Most Wanted" mug shots lists seen in post offices, now online.) This incident, which began with an instant, intuitive insight—"Something's not right here"—is about as good as it gets in spontaneous street policing. The Red Robin robbers—caught red handed.

10

FORWARD PANIC

Our Mission 1 car headed west on SF's main drag, Market Street, near The Castro Theatre at about 8:20 p.m. one evening, with Charley riding shotgun and me at the wheel. Suddenly we heard the sound of an engine repeatedly revving. Five cars ahead, sitting on the streetcar tracks, a black Renault with its lights out cranked the engine, then sped into a quick left turn onto Castro Street, bursting through oncoming traffic. A car with no lights, throttling high and hard, committing multiple right-of-way violations—yes, we wanted to check this one out. We turned a corner and looked ahead to where the Renault sped. Instead of spotting "the revver," we were horrified to see a woman lying motionless in the street. Charley immediately called for an ambulance.

People poured into the scene gesturing angrily and wildly at the mystery car, which was now just completing a U-turn down the street and speeding back directly toward us. The black Renault flew past our car, and I quickly backed up and U-turned our big Ford as Charley grabbed the radio hand set. "Mission 1—in pursuit." The Renault turned right at 17th and headed east. We came around behind it with our reds on and siren sounding—the chase was on. It would be the shortest I've ever experienced.

Mr. Black Renault sped toward a PG&E (Pacific Gas & Electric) utility barricade, behind which lay a three-foot dirt mound situated in front of a wide hole, eight feet deep. The Renault crashed through the barricade and up and over the mound—then disappeared. Within seconds, our mystery man popped up like a jack-in-the-box, running full tilt. I chased him between houses, over fences, through bushes and backyards, down an alleyway, and back toward 17th Street, where I tackled him, dragged him roughly upright, and ran him toward the radio car. We cuffed him up and threw him in the back seat face down.

Siren howling, we went back onto Castro for the injured woman. A movie had just let out at the Castro Theatre, and we faced a mob scene as hundreds of angry, distressed people filled the street. I stopped the car near the downed victim and quickly gave my full attention to the motionless woman. As I knelt over her, I heard shouts from behind me, "Get him! Kill the bastard! Kill the SOB!" Intent on retribution, the mob closed in on our squad car seeking the hit-and-run driver, who was lying in the back seat. Over my right shoulder, I saw three men ripping open the rear door and dragging out the handcuffed prisoner.

I needed backup fast and also needed to keep the mob at bay. Split-second decision: *"Do I pull out my gun and confront the mob, or try to radio for help? If I pull my gun, the people in the crowd might grab it, take me down, and use it against me."* In a millisecond, I'd gone from pursuer and authority to a potential victim of an unruly mob, transformed from social-control agent to potential victim at extreme risk. The tables had turned. I decided to risk a radio call, wondering if I could reach into the car to access the radio handset. I snaked my arm in and barely managed to reach the broadcast microphone. "Mission 1…'406'…Castro Theatre!" It was the ultimate distress call. Reserved for worst-case scenarios, a '406' meant: *"Send immediate, all-out help. I'm in deep trouble; I've lost control; I'm sinking; throw me a life ring."*

Almost immediately I heard a surrounding chorus of sirens, building toward a crescendo—the sweetest sound ever. Backup would arrive quickly, but I still had to keep our arrestee from being torn to pieces by the agitated crowd. Control never came from retreat. I spun around, drew my .38, and pointed it directly at the angry men holding the prisoner half out of the car—a veritable lynching in progress. "Drop him or I will kill you. I mean it. Let him go or you are dead." My resolve was met with shock, hesitation, and piercing stares. Reluctantly they dropped him to the ground and slowly retreated. Sounds of sirens from every direction grew louder and louder as flashing red lights filled the night sky. Squad cars screeched to a halt at all angles, filling the street, doors flying open and officers running to our rescue. Motorcycle cops wove through the crowd revving their engines, breaking up the mob and instigating dispersal.

That evening I'd come face-to-face with the potential for human barbarity, witnessing the brink of a social phenomenon called "Forward Panic," described by author Steven Pinker in *The Better Angels of Our Nature* as the point when "fear turns to rage—men explode in a savage frenzy and beat the enemy senseless—a carnival of barbarity—the common trigger—the isolated enemy. The instinct behind rampages suggests that the human behavioral repertoire includes scripts for violence that lie quiescent and may be cured by propitious circumstances, rather than building up over time like hunger or thirst." Fortunately, the woman who had been hit by the Renault survived. My sense of invulnerability did not.

Girl in the Hallway

We rolled out of the back of Mission Station on a Saturday just after midnight. The radio directed, "Mission 1—to the address 2647 Folsom Street, near 24th Street, opposite the elementary school—a '418.'" Domestic altercations are often tricky. No matter how much information you have, when you arrive, things could be entirely different.

A block and a half from our destination, the radio changed the status of the call from a '418' family fight to a '418 and man with a gun.' Another officer, a one-man unit, advised via radio that he was nearby and would back us up. We pulled up in front simultaneously with the other unit. En route I'd unlocked my shotgun and had it ready. We alighted from our cars and positioned ourselves three across at the front of the address, looking up a flight of twelve stairs toward two front doors fronting a landing. Cautiously ascending the stairs with me in the middle of the group, I had the shotgun pointed directly ahead and upward. Our gaze was fixed on those doors.

Halfway up the stairs, we heard three loud shots from behind one of the doors. The backup officer on my left moved quickly, vaulting over the railing into the driveway ten feet down, abandoning us. He was now safely out of the line of fire, but we had lost our backup. My partner and I continued up the stairs. Suddenly the left door burst open. A man excitedly exited and ran down the stairs, yelling, "He shot her! He shot her!" I leveled the shotgun at the door as the panicked man continued past us. Arriving at the landing, I saw the door was ajar. With the muzzle of the shotgun, I gently pushed the door open. My view of the inside widened until the door stopped, halfway open, blocked by a woman's body. She wasn't moving. Leading, with the shotgun leveled, I stepped over the body, all the while keeping my gaze widely focused, scanning and staying hyperalert to danger. I looked first into a living room to the left of the body. It looked clear. Then I swept my vision straight ahead.

Running down the hallway away from me was a man with a handgun in his right hand. "Halt!" I yelled while targeting the shotgun clearly on him, disengaging its safety. I was ready to fire when the man heeded my call, halted, and slowly began turning around, bringing his gun up toward a "hip-shooting" firing position. A face-off, seemingly unfolding in slow motion, precisely defined each physical action. I started to press the shotgun trigger when a little blond girl in pajamas, maybe seven or eight, darted into the hallway, directly between us, in the line of fire. In the fraction of a second that I had to react, I disengaged the trigger, hoping the gun would not discharge. It did not. I yelled, "Go back in the living room and lie on the floor." She reversed course and scooted away.

The man at the other end of the hallway took advantage of the distraction and ran further into the dwelling and momentarily out of sight. Charley and I followed down the hallway and heard a door slam. It was quickly apparent he had entered the bathroom. I ordered him to open the door and come out with his hands up. He didn't. I braced myself to kick the door in when I heard a gun go off in the bathroom. My mind raced. "Is there a hole in the door? Am I shot?" My left boot crashed the door above the lock. The door splintered open, revealing a man with a bleeding gunshot wound to the chest, lying on the floor face up—with the gun still in his hand.

My foot nudged the gun away. The action seemed over, but the hard work was just beginning. We had two gunshot victims and a complex crime scene. Our "backup" had evaporated. Charley ran to our car and radioed for ambulances. Officers began arriving. San Francisco policemen "covered one another" by rolling toward a potentially dangerous call until the primary assigned unit "Code 4'd" via car radio that the situation was under control.

Fortunately, both victims survived. Part of a lovers' triangle, the woman had been shot three times at the front door, and the shooter had apparently tried to commit suicide in the bathroom. Having faced potential imminent death in the incident, we were stunned that we received only a third-grade meritorious award for our actions. Meanwhile, the "backup" officer who bailed on us was eventually promoted. We never mentioned what he did at the scene. A rather chagrined and subdued Lieutenant Himmelstoss, our watch commander, approached Charley and me and explained what had occurred after our captain put us in for a first-grade award (explanations of administrative decisions were rare). The lieutenant told us an influential police executive on the reviewing board didn't believe the series of threatening events we reported, thinking we'd exaggerated or outright fabricated, so the board simply decided to degrade, invalidate, and deny our reality.

One Lucky Guy

It was 2:00 a.m. at the foot of Twin Peaks. Our Mission 1 radio car was stopped, dead still, at 16th and Castro when a radio call summoned, "Mission 1."

Charley acknowledged, "Mission 1."

"80 Beaver Street: we got a '913.'" An ominous broadcast classification, 913 means *"Investigate: Complaint Unknown."* By pure luck, we were less than two blocks away from the scene. We made a beeline for Beaver, a narrow, angled alley nestled on the far eastern edge of Twin Peaks.

A panicky woman beckoned us along a lengthy, wood-boarded walkway to a front door, saying her husband was cut up and bleeding badly. We funneled through a dim hallway into the living room where an enormous, gray-faced man lay face up on a sofa, not moving, his clothes soaked through with oozing blood. He'd been slashed by razor-sharp, jagged glass, from forehead to ankle, when he crashed through a plate-glass door. He appeared to be bleeding out through virtually every wound. The man could die in minutes—no time to call and wait for an ambulance. We needed to bring him to the hospital ourselves. It was a long haul to the radio car, and I doubted Charley and I could have carried him, even with one of us taking the head and arms and the other at the ankles and feet.

Only one plan came to mind. I ordered Charley to stand at the man's head and the woman to stand at his feet. Facing the middle of the sofa, I went down on my hands and knees. Charley and the woman rolled the six-foot-four, 230-pound victim over my scrunched-down head, onto my shoulders and upper back. I bent backward, experiencing intense pressure on my lower back. I flexed and came up to a forty-five-degree angle, bent slightly upward, staggering slightly, then used every bit of energy and muscle to stand up in a fireman's carry.

With the bleeder draped across my shoulders, I hustled out to the Mission 1 car and dumped him inside. Reaching speeds of fifty to sixty-five miles per hour, we raced east down the hill onto Market Street, siren blaring, emergency lights on, high-intensity spotlight sweeping side to side as we approached intersections, in "Max Code 3" status en route to Central Emergency Hospital. Fortunately, the hospital staff was briefed in advance via radio, and medics with a gurney were awaiting us outside. Our lucky bleeder survived.

A few weeks later, we received a very nice letter from the man's wife, thanking us for saving her husband's life. The treating MD at Central Emergency opined our bleeder wouldn't have survived if we'd waited for an ambulance. The Mission 1 car was in the right place at the right time, and "proper police action" saved a life when stars, planets, and heavenly bodies aligned for one lucky guy.

Rescue by Horse

New Year's Eve is not the easiest time to maintain the general peace, order, and security, yet this was my task on the night preceding January 1, 1962. Positioned on Fifth Street between Mission and Market, I was stationed amid thousands of freewheeling celebrants, many of whom were drunk, some perhaps under the influence of drugs. As we got increasingly close to the midnight hour, people's exuberant behavior was less and less restrained. Appearing slightly frightened and agitated, they pushed, jostled, screamed, jumped up and down, threw confetti, poked one another's party hats, and seemed to be working really hard at having a good time. At least I was getting paid for this exposure.

Circulating on the more-or-less-safe perimeter of the crowd, I maintained a watchful eye, along with several other officers. To my left, toward Market Street, I noticed an oval-shaped opening developing in the midst of a swelling crowd of several hundred people. It likely meant that a person was lying on the ground in the middle of the surrounding celebrants. I proceeded through the crowd, gently pushing toward the opening I had noted, to find a male lying on his back, the apparent victim of a stabbing. Two other officers joined me, and we contemplated what action to take, as we had no radio or other form of communication. The crowd was pushing in, yelling and getting increasingly raucous and menacing, as the unconscious victim bled, edging toward death.

Standing six feet four inches, I was tall enough to see over the crowd toward Market Street, where I noticed a police officer on horseback. I took off my hat and vigorously waved it back and forth, jumping up and down hoping the mounted officer would notice. Turning his steed in our direction and apparently spurring the horse, the rescuer cantered toward us down the middle of Fifth Street, excitedly yelling and waving his hat. All we needed was a bugle call. The crowd separated quickly to allow the horseman through. On scene, the mounted officer moved his horse roughly around, in an exhibition of power, control, and dominance, forcing the crowd away from the victim.

An intoxicated celebrant exercised poor judgment, confronting the mounted officer, who immediately spurred the horse, turning it around, tail toward the offender. In utter amazement, we watched as the horse raised one rear foot, then—BAM—vigorously kicked the drunken challenger in the middle of his chest, sending him soaring through the air. Whoa. As the crowd screamed and scattered, the distraction allowed us to move the victim to a safer location and seek the help of an ambulance crew. Happy New Year.

More Patrollin'

Three years into my police career, I thought seriously about becoming an FBI Agent. I obtained an FBI application, then walked toward the Civic Center area of San Francisco and sat on a bench. Examining the form, I convinced myself the FBI wouldn't ever hire me as an Agent because I wasn't a lawyer or accountant—just not Agent material. I never turned in that application.

Meanwhile, policing by the Golden Gate had a wearing and coarsening effect on many officers. Their demeanor became hardened as they increasingly viewed life in a depressive, defensive, somewhat weary way. The boxy-looking stations had a stark, hard, dirty reality born of unwashed street people, violent offenders, and bad housekeeping. Holding cells were smelly, stuffy, and dank. A festering, ill-defined uneasiness crept over me.

One notoriously drunken patrol sergeant often slept on duty in the rear seat of his parked personal auto. He periodically had to be awakened by a patrolman so he could minimally perform. After one municipal election, "Sergeant Drunk's" political positioning abruptly strengthened, and he was suddenly elevated—zipping past lieutenant and captain ranks—into a position of Director of a major police division.

Attending postgraduate education courses and doing student-teaching during the day, I continued policing at night. While I liked policing better than high-school teaching, being a San Francisco police officer seemed, in the long term, very limiting and negatively defining. Accomplishments, education, and proven ability had little bearing on an officer's chances of promotion or moving into assignments that insured growth, challenge, and greater prestige. Perhaps most pointedly, "old-school" lieutenants generally looked very suspiciously at officers who had attended college.

The politics of promotion to Detective and assignments were tied to a number of ill-defined factors, wrapped up to create what was branded as "juice"—a series of touchstones, a complex web of vague, influential, interpersonal connections, including high school alma mater. As a result, underqualified officers who were held in low esteem but had "juice" would eventually be promoted into investigatory roles with increased responsibility, pay, and growth potential. I candidly acknowledged that my only path to promotion would be years of studying boring, repetitive police procedure books and rules-and-regulations manuals. If successful on the promotional examinations, I might aspire to become that washed-out, baggy-eyed lieutenant "reading the orders" in a toneless voice to a group of distant-eyed, indifferent uniformed officers awaiting their midnight patrol duties.

Six years into policing, my angst was reaching new heights. I was soul-searching, pondering an uninspiring, unfulfilling future when I began working a steady 7:00 p.m. to 3:00 a.m. shift with Fred Kennedy. Fred was driving us up a short, sharply curved driveway from the Hall of Justice basement onto Seventh Street to begin a shift when he casually asked me, in his prominent Irish brogue, "Hey John, ya know what this job qualifies us for?"

Absent-minded and emotionally low, I thought for a few seconds, then answered a bored, "No, Fred."

In a flat voice, Fred replied, "More patrollin'."

Shazam. The dull-toned but insightful exchange was a defining moment, a catalyst for a change of career. Confronting a constrained, limiting future of "more patrollin'" spurred a dawning, stark awareness that personal, immediate action was required. Three years had gone by since I'd decided against applying to the FBI, and now I was even more disillusioned with life as a police officer. I'd been mired down, stuck in a process known as "dwelling"; that is, being "fixated on the current situation, reflecting largely on its negatives, which does not motivate the person to act." [Streep and Bernstein in *Mastering the Art of Quitting*] What next? Seeking any exit strategy, I began qualifying for investigative positions with county district attorney offices, and passed civil service tests for probation officer and state parole agent positions, all of which required a college degree and investigative experience. Anything sounded better than "more patrollin'."

March Forth

Captain Les Dolan, a longtime family friend who proudly wore an FBI National Academy ring, encouraged me, saying, "John, the FBI hires individuals with police investigative backgrounds, college degrees, and other professional experience. Let me make a call for you to the applicant coordinator in the FBI." Dolan assumed the role of mentor—he was pushing aside my blocking demons, offering encouragement, and showing a way forward. In *Making Hope Happen,* Dr. Shane J. Lopez observes that "hope" kicks in when "we reconnect to a meaningful future," and confidence takes hold that "we can make that future our own." Hope emphasizes that "we can get there from here, and underlies purpose-driven action." Hope differs from wishful, fanciful, even positive thinking, in that it's a "realistic pathway to achieving a life enhancing goal."

Now, for the first time, a manager was clearing and smoothing that path, which gave me some semblance of hope. Captain Dolan's mentoring and confidence-building, coupled with his "purpose-driven action," had given me hope—creating and illuminating a realistic "way to get there from here." "Mental imaging" brought clarity of purpose, leading to seemingly achievable pathways. An achievable dream became realistic and might be within reach—becoming an FBI Special Agent.

Dolan set up a screening interview with a Special Agent handling "applicants" who administered the comprehensive testing requirements and conducted my background investigation. He was a marvelous guy, professional, engaging, always keeping me informed of my progress. The FBI presented the opportunity to conduct challenging investigations with a wide variety of complex assignments in a multitude of jurisdictional areas. The Bureau ran on merit and had an outstanding professional reputation under Director J. Edgar Hoover. I awaited word for months. The hiring process was delayed as the FBI continually canceled classes, meanwhile filling limited available new Agent slots with men who'd qualified after me, yet were judged more "perishable"—potentially lost if not hired promptly—whereas I had stable employment.

After waiting a full eighteen months, I finally called Special Agent Anderson and said, "I need to get on with my career, because if I stay on this current course, I'm only eligible to become either a state parole agent or county probation officer." Anderson assured me I was still in the pipeline to become an FBI Special Agent, saying, "Just hang on for a week or so and see what happens." Four days later, I received a letter from FBI Director Hoover offering me an appointment as an FBI Special Agent, effective March 4, 1968, some six months distant, with training beginning in the nation's capital.

Part Three:

The Bureau

The Old Post Office Building—Washington, DC

(source: Library of Congress)

11

HOUSE OF HOOVER

A chilly, gray, overcast sky greeted my late-afternoon arrival at Washington National Airport on Saturday, March 2, 1968. Riding into the District across the Potomac River revealed an endless string of stone-faced government buildings, their facades mirroring overhead clouds. The following day after breakfast at a small counter diner in a chain drugstore, I depleted nervous energy aimlessly walking several miles, scoping out the FBI Building at Tenth and Pennsylvania where I'd report Monday morning, March 4. My reconnoiter found more endless blocks of stone-gray structures and several diners named Hot Shoppe, giving no hint of my future intimate contact with the yet-unrevealed diversity of this churning political cauldron of a city.

Teaming up with a couple of other new Agents, we rented a dilapidated townhouse on New Jersey Avenue SE, in the Capitol Hill neighborhood. It gave us privacy and a vigorous eight-block morning walk to our "Academy"—a single room on the sixth floor of the Old Post Office Building (OPO) at Twelfth and Pennsylvania Avenue NW. A massive edifice, the OPO's dominant presence rose midway between

Capitol Hill and the White House. Its heritage and solidity always impressed me as I navigated its corridors, rode in its "bird cage" elevators (with uniformed operators), admired the rounded interior spaces of its corner turrets, and marveled at its 315-foot-high clock tower. Derided as "old fashioned" from the outset, scarcely used, sometimes abandoned, its 1899 opening ceremonies were marred by a death plunge down an elevator shaft by the District's postmaster general. The OPO exuded strength, security, and staying power, withstanding frequent threats of demolition to become a DC survivor. During Watergate it was home plate to the FBI Washington Field Office's C-2 (Miscellaneous Crimes) Squad.

A month into training, on the morning of April 5, 1968, I looked out the upper-level front windows of the OPO as chaos erupted below. The day before, Martin Luther King Jr. was assassinated in Memphis, Tennessee, and riots engulfed the nation's capital. Perched safely on the sixth floor, my classmates and I watched men smash the large plate-glass windows of Kaufman's Men's Store and emerge hauling out heaps of merchandise. No police interceded to stop the burglary in progress, and I mused out loud, "We should do something about that." Our instructors told us not to involve ourselves and suspended classes, ordering us home for a three-day hiatus. Calm came days later only after army combat vehicles appeared and soldiers seized control of the streets—a jarring reminder of the crucial role of peacekeepers bringing and insuring stability to the fragile social order.

Days later we headed thirty-six miles south of the District to begin three weeks of training at the FBI firearms ranges located in the remote western fringes of the Marine base at Quantico, Virginia. Our residence, Hodgemuth Hall, was a two-story brick structure located several miles away on the base's "main side." The ground floor contained administrative offices and a day room for relaxing, reading, and watching TV. At a formal dining hall (jacket and tie mandatory), uniformed waiters served us meals at oval tables. The sleeping quarters upstairs consisted of army bunks so close together that when one of us turned over in his sleep, his arm would hit the next guy. Outside in the hallway, each trainee had a narrow, six-foot-high steel locker for clothing and toiletries, making mornings beyond a scrum. The mixed cultural signals struck me— downstairs we dined like Southern gentlemen; upstairs we slept in a homeless shelter.

The firearms guys on the ranges did a superb job with revolver, Thompson submachine gun, and shotgun basics. Hogan's Alley was an innovative, interactive, "live-fire" environment where we walked a movie-lot mock-up of moving, spontaneous street engagements featuring "shoot or don't shoot" decision-making challenges. Driver training consisted of a basic ride-along to determine whether we could start, stop, steer, and generally guide a vehicle: pursuit and felony stop procedures weren't included.

Stories abounded of New York City guys who couldn't drive, as they apparently spent their lives on subways and buses. Years later I was riding south on I-95 with a New York native, Tom Baker, in his VW Bug. As the engine screamed painfully, I mentioned, "It has another gear."

Surprised, he replied, "It does?"

I advised, "Put in the clutch and hold it." As he clutched, I gently shifted the tortured vehicle into third gear, and you could almost hear it sigh in relief.

Our twelve-week course taught us the basics of Bureau procedure, law, rules, and regulations, ending with a slight shrug and forced laugh from our training guide. An instructor handed us our FBI credentials and gold badges, admonishing us to get out of DC "before sunset." That way, being officially 'en route' to our first field office, any trouble that might befall us "would be the responsibility of our new Special Agent in Charge." Unlike today's new Agents, who receive their FBI credentials individually from the Director on stage before invited guests in a beautiful theater on the Quantico campus, we had no graduation ceremony—a holdover of 1930s minimalism still practiced in the Bureau of the late 1960s.

At last, training was over and the "real" FBI beckoned. I exited the Twelfth Street side of the OPO on June 6, 1968, thinking, "Thank God I'll never see this place again."

Destination Dallas

I flew home to San Francisco to say my good-byes to family and friends. From there, I hopped in my little, blue Porsche and headed across town for my symbolic final fill-up at the Texaco Station at 16th Street and South Van Ness, which offered a "special discount" private gas pump for cops, embossed with an SFPD star, courtesy of the dealer. Now, that's appreciation. While my eight and a half years as a cop were behind me, I felt validated enough to indulge this perk one last time.

While filling my tank, I reflected on the ceremonial dinner my former peers had given me at the El Patio Ballroom prior to my resigning. No brass attended, and the best I ever received from Chief Cahill was a tellingly blunt "No" to my request for a three-year leave of absence to pursue my FBI opportunity. Apparently he viewed me as a deserter. Inspector Dick Castro, who happened to also be at the gas station, spied me and offered a hearty hello. He said he admired my qualifying as an FBI Special Agent and wished me the best. It made me feel just a little proud as I headed east across the Bay Bridge, my hometown disappearing behind me, and a long, solitary drive of 2,500 miles ahead.

Straight down Highway 99 through the Central Valley and across the Mojave Desert brought me to a stop at the Arizona-California border. Rural radio stations kept me company as the following day

I ascended through a mottled, reddening, rocky desert, with woodsy mountains beckoning beyond. Flagstaff provided a plateau and a beautiful, tree-filled respite. I crossed Arizona and the open spaces of New Mexico, both somewhat mirroring California's Mohave Desert, and then endured miles of semiarid sameness until reaching a large truck stop near the Texas line. It seemed OK for an overnighter.

The following morning was to be a dash for the finish line at Dallas. Heading straight east brought me through Amarillo, a place once described to me by Jim "Jump With" Gump, our gym teacher at Quantico, as the only place where you can be "up to your backside in mud and have sand blowing in your face." From there, I angled down and southeast under threatening skies. At about 9:15 a.m., the radio was increasingly interrupted by static as the announcer began warning of "tornado activity in the vicinity of Clyde." Hmm, didn't I just see a sign for Clyde a few minutes ago?

There on the skyline, quite clearly getting bigger, I saw a twisting, gray-black funnel. The wind started picking up. I stopped quickly and scrambled down the roadside embankment. At the bottom of the ditch, I pressed my prone body into a crevice, which I hoped would provide protection, wondering if I'd ever reach my first FBI office. Thankfully, the tornado passed at a safe distance, yet visions lingered of this zigzagging vortex of destruction.

The Texas landscape seemed an endless recycled mile, interspersed with occasional pumping oil derricks. A little bustle, a hint of vehicular congestion, pop-up suburban housing tracts, and a signature mass of lighted skyscrapers ahead signaled entry into the "Dallas-Fort Worth Metroplex." A motel on Dallas's outskirts housed me for the night.

The following morning, after a short wait in a receptionist's area, I was ushered into the office of my SAC (Special Agent in Charge). J. Gordon Shanklin was a respected, intelligent leader who had directed the investigation of President Kennedy's assassination in 1963. A chain smoker, his concentration was so focused and intense that, unbeknownst to him, hot, burning ash occasionally fell from his lip-secured cigarette, burrowing holes in his jacket lapels and tie. En route to major cases, he'd routinely stop to procure a carton of fresh cigarettes. Shanklin offered a pleasant welcome, follow-up small talk, and a directive that I'd fulfill the duties of a "runner" on his squad of experienced Agents. It appeared I was being idled for the present.

My initiation into the Dallas Field Office was jarring and a bit bizarre. Introduced as "the new guy from California," I was eyed somewhat suspiciously, and seemed to be minimally tolerable. There was no desk available, so I shuttled about carrying a clunky, outdated, ugly brown leather government-issued briefcase. The "SAC's Squad" allegedly was composed of former FBI officials who had been demoted, or as we say in the Bureau, "busted" down to lower rank. They seemed seriously consumed by their own work. However, there was none for me. I hung around, getting occasional tidbits. When an extra guy was needed, I received the call.

Deep in the Heart

One assignment had me picking up a couple of mug shots from the Dallas Police Department and racing 175 miles across the flat plains at ninety miles per hour (stopped twice by Texas Highway Patrol) to a major bank robbery (BR) scene. Arriving in Woodson with my much-needed mug shots, it seemed like I was dropping into a B-western movie set. Wooden, plank sidewalks bordered a dusty, dirt main street flanked with small businesses. Occupied rocking chairs were scattered in front of stores.

My aim was directly set on a group of obvious law enforcers milling about. Various styles of cowboy hats adorned the heads of assembled

Texas lawmen, consisting of a town constable, county deputies, and the ever-present top dog of Texas peacekeepers, a legendary State Ranger. Word had it one Ranger showed up in East Texas at Paris to assist locals with a roiling labor strike at a Campbell's soup plant. Locals questioned the dispatched, lonely Ranger: "What, no help? You're it?" His terse reply: "One riot, one Ranger."

To a man, clean jeans without cuffs were a given; these were draped over polished cowboy boots, some of which had spurs. Filling out the Lone Star motif seemed to require a string tie with polished stone clip and a prominent buckle centered on a hand-tooled, wide, and thick leather belt, holding a full-sized, 1911 Colt .45 semi-auto—the handgun of choice. That destroyer usually was prominently displayed and instantly accessible, holstered a bit high, resting comfortably against a hip. Texas is a huge expanse, and lawmen routinely worked alone, long distances from backup. Nobody missed that needed, intimidating message.

My critical mug shots in the hands of the FBI's key guy, I hung around until it was obvious whatever I might offer was not needed. A slower ride back to Dallas caused me to mull over my new career—out there somewhere must be assignments and opportunities, which could drive me forward.

Texas is huge—covering that vast landscape requires independent, self-sufficient cops. Backup, taken for granted in some cities, was not to be had, rare, or a long way away. Dallas detectives operated in a typical city environment, but dressed and adorned themselves in replica fashion of what their country brethren wore. Dallas west to the New Mexico line was cowboy territory: West Texas. Conversely, heading east, a motorist was funneled directly into successive town squares, each featuring a statue of a horse-mounted military officer—a Confederate veteran of the Civil War.

A tall figure, dressed in a dark suit, with regular tie and business hat, would be Mr. Bookout—the FBI bank robbery "coordinator" from Dallas. Each FBI field division had one, and he was duly accorded earned respect. In addition to working actual robberies, he was responsible for spotting robbery patterns and trends, circulating enough to establish and maintain the FBI's dominant footprint throughout the territory as the sure-fire, go-to bank robbery or "BR guy."

Undesirable Trends

On another assignment, I joined some clerks in driving deactivated, stripped-out Bureau cars ("Bu-cars") to the General Services Administration for public auction. Not exactly intense, high-profile assignments. In early July, the Division came "under inspection," a dreaded event. The Inspection Division out of Headquarters would ferret out "Undesirable Trends" (UT): mistakes, oversights, and unacceptable behavior. It seemed "administrative" errors could always be found—official "letters of censor" would document failings, and discipline could be quick and severe. I figured I'd be safe in this inspection because I hadn't yet "done anything"—recalling Police Wisdom: minimal engagement = minimal performance = minimal exposure to criticism.

I was sent to a local Oldsmobile dealer as a shuttle driver to pick up air-conditioned rides the dealer was "loaning" for the visiting "rats." I thought it a bit strange that a super straight outfit like the Bureau would be borrowing from a local business, but "strange" would shortly intensify. The chief inspector had a florid, beaming complexion above a fleshy, beefy body. Being a native San Francisco cop made me expertly qualified to spot a heavy drinker. Several mornings, we noticed he appeared unsteady, wobbling a bit.

Just after the midpoint of the three-week inquisition, we were told that at 9:00 a.m. there would be an "All-Agents Conference." I stood rearward with my back against the radio-room glass. Up front, our SAC announced that the chief inspector had been promoted to SAC of the Oklahoma City (OKC) office and would depart immediately. This was met with mild applause, followed by perfunctory remarks about impending cooperation between Dallas and OKC. Oklahoma City's newly anointed SAC unsteadily swayed and bobbed before finally getting a grip and acknowledging the announcement, with slightly slurred speech and glazed eyes. This guy definitely had a "heat on." As I clasped that dog of a briefcase with both hands, I felt concern that one of the worst attributes I recalled from the SFPD, drinking on duty, might also be part of the FBI. Fortunately, this guy was an outlier.

Going Rogue

Inspections could be nerve-wracking, and it was inevitable that I wouldn't remain under the radar forever. Several Dallas Agents and Clerks told me I'd be driving through "groves of beautiful woods" on the way to my upcoming stint in Paris, East Texas, near the Oklahoma-Arkansas border. Growing up in Northern California, I was accustomed to groves of towering redwoods and robust oaks, and thus buzzed right through Texas's version of "woods," without recognition. Everything's bigger in Texas, except the trees. Following my three-week engagement, I was transferred to the Fort Worth Resident Agency, a suboffice thirty-five miles west of Dallas. It would be my home for the next eight months.

Our leader, B. Tom Carter, was a quiet, unassuming, gentlemanly FBI veteran known to be liked and respected by J. Edgar. Word had it that while Tom was working at FBI Headquarters in DC, he asked to go home to Texas. The Director not only sent him to Fort Worth, but made him its Chief. Tom was a member of a local wealthy founding family who established and funded the world-class Amon Carter Museum of American Art.

It was just my luck that the Dallas Division came under inspection again in May 1969, prior to my departure for Washington, DC. A chief inspector named Richard Rogue roared through our little Fort Worth office with an aide as we stood nervously at attention beside our file cabinets. He vigorously slammed open a file drawer of mine with such force that a Bureau "serial," or document, became dislodged, flying into the air. It floated back and forth, gently descending, as everyone looked horrified.

Rogue reacted, flailing, in a repeated grasp-snap aerial dogfight, as the offender eluded him like a loose ball on the basketball court. He finally snagged and read the offending floater. Hearts pounded, pulses throbbed, faces reddened. "Whew!" It wasn't mine: it was from an old, inconsequential case. Next, he eyed my files. A slight smile creased his angry face as he noted their "neatness." Praise, representing attention, from the chief inspector, however, might not be a good thing. Rogue moved on to another target. Revolvers with open, unloaded cylinders were on every desk for inspection. At that moment, if anybody attacked our office, we would be defenseless. (Ten years later, in a small, two-man office, Agents had their guns locked securely in their desks—following protocol—when a disgruntled citizen came in through an unlocked door and shot and killed them both. The rule was quickly revised.)

Inspecting the weapons, Rogue picked up Tom's, noting it was an aberrant .32 caliber—everyone in the Bureau carried .38s. In a loud, edgy voice, Rogue demanded an explanation as to how Tom could have a Bureau-issued .32. Tom politely shrugged his shoulders and mildly said he didn't know. Authoritatively, Rogue ordered his aide to "call the Bureau" and get to the bottom of this abnormality. Within the hour, it had been determined that two other people in the FBI had .32's—J. Edgar Hoover and his longtime number-two man, Clyde Tolson. Rogue apologized profusely and backtracked furiously: Tom could keep his .32.

Months later, after I'd left Dallas and moved to the FBI's Washington, DC, Field Office (WFO), I was sipping java with colleagues at the Cuban Coffeehouse across the street from the Old Post Office building. The gossipy morning lead story was a "Wives' Revolt" that engulfed, overran, and unseated the imperious Rogue, who'd become Honolulu SAC. He apparently rode so roughshod over Hawaiian-based Agents that a group of wives protested to Bureau Headquarters, and Rogue was "voted off the island."

Working Capitol

The Dallas ASAC was a pleasant man who addressed any first office Agent by the moniker "Tiger." I happened to be in the Dallas office when he announced, with his customary smiling friendliness, "Tiger, you've been transferred to Washington." I'd be back in the Old Post Office Building (OPO).

All "Tigers" were formally and informally known as "first office Agents," quite similar to rookie status within police departments. Bureau policy was firm—after one year of service, "Tigers" were transferred to their more-or-less permanent assignment, a second office. Like your initial posting, that second office could be anywhere. I was excited to learn I would be headed to Washington, D.C.—a vibrant, pulsating, diverse international city awash with intrigue.

OFFICE OF THE DIRECTOR

UNITED STATES DEPARTMENT OF JUSTICE

FEDERAL BUREAU OF INVESTIGATION

WASHINGTON, D.C. 20535

October 13, 1969

PERSONAL

Mr. John W. Minderman
Federal Bureau of Investigation
Washington, D. C.

Dear Mr. Minderman:

   In recognition of your noteworthy performance in connection with the investigation and apprehension of ████████ ████████ ████████, one of the subjects of a Bank Robbery case, I want to commend you.

   Your skill and ingenuity in assisting in the arrest of ████████ contributed substantially to the success realized in this endeavor. I want you to know of my appreciation for your effective efforts.

     Sincerely yours,

     J. Edgar Hoover

OFFICE OF THE DIRECTOR

UNITED STATES DEPARTMENT OF JUSTICE

FEDERAL BUREAU OF INVESTIGATION

WASHINGTON, D.C. 20535

December 11, 1969

PERSONAL

Mr. John W. Minderman
Federal Bureau of Investigation
Washington, D. C.

Dear Mr. Minderman:

Your performance in detaining an individual who was attempting to assault police officers was excellent and it is a pleasure to take this opportunity to commend you.

The prompt and aggressive manner in which you and an associate handled this matter was responsible for the arrest of this man by the local police. I certainly appreciate your noteworthy efforts.

Sincerely yours,

J. Edgar Hoover

12

SHOTGUN IN THE RAIN

Upon arrival at the FBI Washington Field Office in May 1969, I sat in the SAC's office waiting to meet my supervisor, sensing the atmosphere was a bit strained. In walked Charley Johnson—tall, thin, with slicked-back black hair and chewing gum with some intensity. He led the C-2 Squad and would be my new boss. I don't recall ever seeing him smile or exhibit the slightest sense of humor. We exited the room together bantering with some guy small talk. I came to appreciate and respect his even-handed, pragmatic leadership.

The C-2 "bullpen," the open area where the Agents roosted behind gray, steel desks, faced the Twelfth Street side of the Old Post Office building (OPO), our gray stone fortress. Agent Jim Vellos droned into a dictating machine as his cigarette smoke curled upward toward twelve-foot ceilings. Usually a new arrival chooses any empty desk, but not in my case. Johnson pointed and intoned, "That'll be your desk." I noticed Vellos and a couple other Agents looking my way with quizzical, mildly concerned expressions.

Later I learned my notorious desk formerly belonged to SA Woodruff, who was killed along with Agent Palzano by bank robber Billy Austin Bryant on January 8, 1969. The FBI called in a massive police presence for the manhunt and cordoned off fifty square blocks in southeast Washington, DC, going block to block, house to house, alley to alley, to track down the killer. I'd have to break whatever spell hovered around the "death desk." The first couple of weeks, I acquainted myself with these men, who were accepting and helpful yet reserved and cautious. Friendships took a while to cultivate.

Happy Apps

Two full squads of FBI Agents labored on the assembly lines of checking and verifying backgrounds of potential federal workers and appointments. Seen as dull drudgery, held in low esteem, and not likely to generate much career leverage, these jobs consistently got the fresh faces arriving at WFO. The new arrivals were sentenced to six months to a year in purgatory on "Happy Apps" (applicants). If low status wasn't enough, it was rumored our exiled brethren suffered additional indignities: placement on the OPO's uppermost floor with nesting attic pigeons and a leaky roof, insuring daily cleaning and wet-season challenges. Everyone except me did time there before becoming eligible for a spy-catching or criminal-chasing slot.

A fellow Agent attended Florida State University on an athletic scholarship. His nifty cuts on the football field and home-run blasts apparently didn't translate into a professional athletic career. After policing in Oakland, California, he eventually found his way into the Bureau. Oakland PD recruited nationally on college campuses and had many college-educated cops. More than a few joined the FBI, eventually ascending the hierarchy, seemingly constituting a fraternity and generating their own "juice." He seemed particularly blessed, with his athletic prowess, sharp intellect, and an earned, genuine street-confident reputation.

I'd never paid much attention to the fact that I skipped "Happy Apps" and was quietly appreciative for the apparent oversight. However, this ate at him. During one morning coffee break, I noticed his brooding, unhappy, pockmarked face staring intently at me. "Hey, Min, I've got to ask you something. How come you never had to do any time on Happy Apps?"

I replied truthfully, "I don't know."

He bore in with his most withering, lock-on, "You-expect-me-to-believe-that?" stare. He pressed harder, "Nobody skips Happy Apps."

"Honestly, I really don't know," I responded. "It just happened, but if you're wondering why you had to do it and I didn't...I've some ideas."

Surrounding Agents suppressed little smiles. The Agent bit. "Let's have it."

I replied, "Well, it could have to do with the fact that you came from a podunk, small, barely significant police department, and I did my policing in a major department."

Incredulous, he shot back, "No way! Oakland's way better than San Francisco."

I retreated. "But that probably isn't it. My guess is that they pulled our personnel files, and my scores on all the physical tests exceeded yours."

His face hardened and reddened—he was clearly aggravated. The indignity! In a low, deliberate voice, with a tinge of dime-novel menace, he voiced, "You've got to be kidding!"

This Agent and I came close, but never really bonded. He went on to a coveted spot on "91s"—bank robberies—and just when things were really coming together for him, he got lured away by what looked like a hot opportunity. Another Agent with real juice—family money—and a Phi Beta Kappa from the University of Chicago, lined up an investigative appointment for himself on Florida Representative Claude Pepper's "crime committee." The juiced Agent let him know there were a couple of additional slots open, and he resigned from the FBI for political toil.

Six months or so later, the committee and the jobs disappeared. Supposedly, the former-Agent operated a tow truck for a while before he was accepted back into the Bureau, thus forevermore being dubbed a "retread." The second time around, he ascended like a rocket by combining new smarts gained from hard experience and late-blooming maturity.

The Agent's nagging question about my evasion of Happy Apps servitude was never answered, but I eventually figured out a "probable." The loss of SA Woodruff four months prior created the need for an Agent with "street smarts." My tough years of police work had me in the right place at the right time—my inquisitor was just a little late.

The Importance of Drinking Coffee

Legendary Hoover stories were shared by veteran FBI Agents over early morning coffee at the Cuban Coffeehouse, located across the street from the OPO in Washington, DC—an oasis frequented by a mix of FBI types, including Headquarters personnel of various ranks and working Street Agents from the WFO. All of us were "illegals" in that we were flagrantly violating the Bureau rule against drinking coffee on duty. The reasoning behind the rule: if you're drinking coffee, you're not working. Flouting the rule added a bit of roguish flavor to our meetings, which were strictly happenstance. Generally, you sat with whatever group had a chair available when you entered. The HQ personnel knew everything going on nationally and internationally, and WFO

Agents had the ground-level take on the capital. Here we could relax and share the latest gossip, scoops, and trends of everything Bureau.

The Orange Tree

Director Hoover enjoyed visiting Miami. The weather, I imagine, appealed to him, in addition to the availability of horse racetracks. As the Director, he was able to combine business and pleasure. Returning to Miami one year for his annual inspection visit, the Director stayed at a motel in a ground-floor room he had previously occupied. On this trip, when he opened the drapes, he noted the absence of a beautiful orange tree, which had been on view during a prior year. The mere mention of his disappointment was enough to prompt Agents to aggressively mobilize. They hustled up a suitable orange tree and made sure that it was planted in the Director's line of sight, so he would see it when he opened his billowing drapes the following morning.

Raise the Floor

In another episode, a major manufacturer of bathroom fixtures made a gift to the Director of one of its "high-end" toilets—allegedly a thank you for superior FBI performance in a kidnapping case. The Director mentioned to his housecleaner that his feet dangled uncomfortably in the air while he was seated on the new commode. The observation was passed on to the Bureau's Exhibits section, which ordinarily made all manner of scale models to depict crime scenes used in trials. Agents mulled over the dilemma. "Should we raise the floor, or lower the toilet?" Potential solutions were deeply pondered over coffee. I don't know which approach was adopted, but rest assured that dangling legs no longer annoyed our Director, closing the lid on this game of thrones.

No Left Turns

One of the experienced Agents in Fort Worth, Joseph Schott, wrote a couple of books, one of which was entitled *No Left Turns*, a series of anecdotes about quirky FBI behavior. The title depicted an incident that happened to Director Hoover while he was on an inspection tour in the Dallas Division. It seems that while the Director's car was stopped, awaiting clearance to make a safe left turn, it was struck in the rear. Since the proximate cause of getting rear-ended was stopping to make a left turn, the Director concluded that it was unnecessarily dangerous to conduct such a maneuver. Thus, he commanded that in all future automobile excursions, while Mr. Hoover was in the rear seat, the FBI driver would make no left turns.

Watch the Borders

We all knew the Director was the only person in the FBI who was allowed to write with blue ink. After reviewing one particular memo, the Director sent it back down the chain of command with prominent blue-inked orders to "Watch the Borders!" No further explanation was offered on the memo. Agents, it was assumed, could always decipher the message and "take the proper action." The chain of command attempted to interpret the edict. Could this be attached to an ongoing investigation? No clear answer emerged. Compelled to respond, the "brain trust" eventually decided that Hoover must want the FBI to watch the United States' contiguous borders with Mexico and Canada. Dozens of FBI Agents were dispatched to our national borders to keep watch—but for what? Well, Agents always knew "it" when they saw "it." After two or three days of unproductive watchfulness, the brain trust eventually decided the Director's order didn't refer to geographic borders—he was merely concerned about the formatting of the memo. The text apparently ran too close to the edges of the paper, leaving insufficient space for the Director's blue-penned instructions.

Smoking Jacket

Agents ignored the Director's wishes, or incurred his wrath, at their peril. The original FBI Headquarters at Tenth and Pennsylvania was a building where Agents moving up the hierarchy could, without warning, come upon top FBI officials when walking the halls. One relatively lowly supervisor found himself in an elevator about to puff a lit cigar. As the doors opened, he spied Director Hoover and his ever-present Number Two, Clyde Tolson, about to enter. Mortified, the supervisor quickly stuffed the lit cigar into his suit pocket, attempting to crush it out by pressing the side of the coat, and burning a large hole in his jacket in the process. As news of this career-saving action circulated, the supervisor later explained that, overall, such action was warranted and certainly prudent, as destroying a suit jacket was a lot cheaper than what might have happened to his career.

Unlucky Ducklings and a Tattooed Monkey

Back in the OPO, Supervisory Special Agent (SSA) Johnson assigned me as the contact/liaison Agent to the National Zoological Police, headquartered at the bottom of Rock Creek Park. Days later I found myself wandering around among the caged animals, searching for police headquarters. I eventually did my song and dance, letting them know that if any government property was stolen, I was their "go-to" guy.

Success came my way when the zoo cops notified me that three ring-tailed ducklings were missing. Would we open a case? Although the little paddlers might already be in somebody's backyard pond or homemade soup, I assured them with gusto that the FBI would help get their ducks in order. Weeks later, the zoo's largest monkey was hijacked. Apparently he was worth $1,500, and I went into high gear, teletyping all FBI offices up and down the East Coast. Fortuitously, the monkey had an identifying tattoo. Agents acting on a tip recovered the kidnapped primate up for sale in a Philadelphia pet shop. They faxed us a photo of the monkey, looking really happy, posed on a Bureau desk between two Agents. The picture became a favored exhibit icebreaker, as I'd explain the two figures on the perimeter were the Agents.

Movable Type

Months later, I felt grounded as I cranked out the Bureau equivalent of criminal assembly-line work. The big-theft items of the era were IBM Selectric typewriters. By the dozens, they disappeared, and we recovered few. Eventually, an alert GSA (General Services Administration) building guard provided a car license (or as was said in DC, a "tag number"). Our vigorous background work identified a very active theft ring, headed by a man named Crumfield.

We planned to take down the ring by catching them red-handed, beginning surveillance at 3:00 a.m. one morning across the southeast DC border in suburban Maryland. This kind of caper is awash with unpredictability. We would follow an identified car, but we had no way of knowing where we would end up or what might transpire if or when our suspect arrived at his destination of theft opportunity and beyond. We anticipated theft activity, so this effort would require improvisation.

I devised and utilized a six-step decision-making process, which I dubbed "Adjustments on the Fly": (1) identify unforeseen breakdowns in the plan; (2) instantly devise a creative solution; (3) unhesitatingly execute the action; (4) coordinate subsequent group response; (5) operate under time pressure; (6) be flexible to readjust.

There were no "special operations groups," with undercover cars or specialized training during my era—just eight Street Agents: similar looking white guys, seated in two-man government-issued cars from Detroit's standard low end, with a lot of aerials sticking out all over. I thus affected a disguise, dressing as a factory laborer. Another Agent and I were following the primary suspect, but despite my disguise, he "made" us immediately. He stopped his vehicle and sat watching in the darkness to see how we might respond—were we really the cops?

Our grand plan was in danger of going into the dumper at the get-go. After several long seconds, I jumped out of my car and ran to the bad guy's car. His side window was open, so I reached through and firmly grabbed him by his lapels, dragging him out bodily until his lower abdomen rested on the sill, his arms stuck within the window frame. He looked scared, he undoubtedly felt vulnerable, and his eyes got big.

In my best affected Southern drawl, I profanely told him he was blocking my passage to work, and he better get moving—pronto. I shoved him back in with a piston-like thrust. Intimidation produces fear and distraction, which generates thoughtlessness. He sped away, shaken up, his personal radar shattered. Without looking back to see if we were tailing him, he drove into the District, where he went directly to the Commerce Department building, a block away from our office, and stole—guess what?—not one, but two, IBM Selectrics. Ah, timing.

Our surveillance effort became easier as we drove through morning traffic, which provided blending cover and happenstance concealment. Laser concentration was required to anticipate and compensate for decreased maneuverability. Teamwork was at its utmost, as our group was always one red light away from being unmasked, or one inept maneuver from being "made."

At a steel-girdered railroad bridge, which spanned New York Avenue, NE, we watched him park by a working dairy and hustle into a shack that was perched on a rocky outcropping, at the bridge abutment, just below the main Baltimore & Ohio train tracks. A couple of guys came out and helped unload the federal booty. By now, it was about two in the afternoon. We had exited our cars and scattered afoot, scoping out the thieves' roost. Our notoriously unpredictable handheld radios were running out of charge, and so were we, without rest, breakfast, or lunch. Alas, my radio crapped out. We needed to generate traction. Time again for "adjustments on the fly."

To evaluate potential responses, I needed a close-up view of the robbers' hideout, so I ran across New York Avenue, a churning, heavily traveled, divided thruway, hearing many protesting honking horns. I hustled over the sidewalk and jumped up on a loading platform of the dairy, startling the workers with my appearance—tall, unshaven, scruffy-looking, wearing old jeans and a plaid shirt. I ran through the dairy shouting "FBI" while waving my credentials and gold badge.

At the rear, from another loading platform, I peered out toward the roost. About three feet below me, at the end of the railroad spur, were two members of the gang. They were now walking right toward me, each carrying a stolen Selectric. If they sensed an imminent bust, they would drop the typewriters and run, so I had to act quickly, freezing them with decisive action. I jumped down, flashed the gold FBI badge, and strong-voiced orders, confronting them at gunpoint. They offered no resistance.

Walking them back to the elevated shack, I was joined by other Agents. We then searched the shack, recovering more evidence, which allowed us to take down the hideout and bust the entire gang. We earned convictions all around, and our casework withstood a challenge all the way through the Federal Appellate Court. The pen may be mightier than the sword, but a typewriter is no match for adjustments on the fly, quick decisive action, and a gun.

Perfect Prints

Bank robberies are inherently dangerous, not just because guns are used, but because most of these actions are poorly planned and executed. Bank robbers don't think much about the details and the requirements for successful robbery. Their actions seem to be spontaneous and lack even basic plans for disguise and security against being identified. Many individuals have been killed or wounded in such crimes.

One morning, a robbery took place in downtown DC at a Riggs National Bank on Seventh Street just north of Pennsylvania Avenue. The bank had a beautiful, ornate, cathedral-like black marble interior, probably built in the 1920s, complete with polished counters of black granite with variegated streaks of gray.

The robber entered the bank, whipped out a gun, fired a shot into the ceiling, and announced, "This is a robbery!" quickly getting everyone's attention. It looked like a classic "takeover" robbery: a shot in the ceiling proclaims purposefulness and demonstrates lethal potential—very intimidating. The robber—an agile athlete—continued his dramatics by making a run at an end counter of the aforementioned granite, vaulting over, and landing behind the teller cages, where he rambled about, cleaning out the cash drawers.

In showing off his athleticism, the robber failed to adequately guard himself against identification. Ungloved during his vault over the counter, he placed his left hand and full palm on the marble surface. In doing so, he sequentially "rolled" (perfectly embossed) all five fingerprints, with a beautifully clear, body weighted, full palm print impressed on the countertop. You couldn't have gotten a better set of complete prints if you were applying for an FBI Agent position.

In fact, all five fingers with a palm are officially called "major case prints." Our robber also looked directly into a surveillance camera, giving us a full facial and pivoting smartly for landing; he was considerate enough to add a beautiful, portrait-quality shot of his profile. If that wasn't enough, as he vaulted the counter, his wallet, complete with a plethora of identification, including his driver's license with current address and credit cards, dislodged from his rear pocket, hit the counter, and conveniently landed on the floor. He was blissfully unaware of this loss.

Zoning Out

At eleven o'clock one morning, our team of four Agents parked our car on Twelfth Street near Pennsylvania Avenue and proceeded into our office for a paperwork blitz. One of the Agents, "Handsome Dan" Mahan, wasn't feeling well, and decided to remain in the car. His plan was to relax, listen to the radio, and perhaps shut his eyes and just zone out, while staying marginally attentive. The three of us left in disgust to do our paperwork. While we were in the office upstairs diligently working on paper, the Agent in question was relaxed in the back of the FBI car, carrying out his mission.

Suddenly the radio came alive, advising all units a bank robbery was committed in the vicinity of Twelfth and E Streets Northwest—just a couple of blocks from the relaxing Agent. It was getting close to the noon hour, and the streets were filled with pedestrians hustling along Pennsylvania Avenue. Alerted from his doze, the newly energized Agent sprang to life and began scanning the area for the fleeing robber, described as wearing mismatched unusual clothing of vibrant colors: "He's wearing a green, pork-pie hat, purple trousers, a yellow sports jacket with brown shoes, and carrying a black leather attaché case." Certainly an individual wearing this kind of outfit would stand out among the tourists and conservatively dressed federal office workers strolling about the area.

Just then, Handsome Dan spied the malefactor. The robber was moving quickly, carrying the designated attaché case directly down Twelfth Street. Conveniently, the robber crossed wide Pennsylvania Avenue and continued in closer proximity to the Agent's car. Dan sprang out and confronted the robber, who offered no resistance and complied with orders to place his hands palms down on the hood while he was searched, and the Agent found and confiscated his gun. With the robber bound by handcuffs and under control, the three of us arrived and assisted by opening the attaché case. Therein was a complete cash drawer containing the stolen bank money. When the case was written up, Dan provided a slightly different explanation for his presence at the apprehension scene; nevertheless he was bestowed an award for diligent attention to duty by the director.

Doth Protest

Undercover wasn't my usual role. However, one evening I abruptly transitioned while monitoring a raging antiwar demonstration at Dupont Circle. A "protester" was using a commercial-grade metal slingshot, with ball bearings as missiles, in repeated attempts to seriously injure uniformed riot cops who were surging back and forth with protesters in seemingly endless attempts to occupy and control ground, like two aggressive dance troupes charging and retreating.

Sling-shot man was way too dangerous. Dressed down, I easily slipped into the crowd and worked my way close to the ball-bearing buster. He consistently placed himself in the vanguard, so I decided to time a "hit, grasp, and run" plan just as his forward momentum crested. I grasped him and succeeded in running his panicked, struggling body toward the mass of cops, all the while yelling, "FBI Special

Agent," hoping I wouldn't be struck by the descending end of a police baton. The cops took the offender and must have notified the FBI, as I soon after received a "personal" letter from Director Hoover, noting that my "prompt and aggressive manner in handling this incident was excellent" and that he "appreciated and commended" my "noteworthy efforts."

Years earlier in San Francisco, I'd witnessed my fair share of all kinds of "demos." Arriving for a 2:00–10:00 p.m. shift, Sgt. Jack Southern told me to dress quickly and immediately bring my patrol car up to ground level. "What's going on?" I hustled up, eventually backing my car into an accessible spot at about 1:30 p.m. In the main office just off the parking lot, shotguns were stacked high on a counter with cases of ammunition nearby. Was I going to war?

Southern was all business. "Pop the trunk, throw all the shotguns in, and put the ammo in the rear seat area. Get out to Third and Newcombe as fast as possible. There's a riot." I guess I'd miss that "break-in" first cup of coffee. Per orders, three dozen long guns were literally thrown into the trunk, and about ten cases of ammo heaved into the rear seat area. The car decidedly tilted, high-end front.

Off I went to 3rd Street, then across Channel Street drawbridge— adjacent to present-day SF Giant's ballpark stadium. It would be a straight mile plus run to my destination—or maybe not. Immediately in view ahead filling 3rd Street I saw scattered groups of distressed, angry people. It looked like I was facing the outer pockets of the protesting rioters. My path looked difficult, if not totally blocked.

Decision time mandated a few seconds of reflection. I had a big Ford 390: on went all the reds as I took the middle of the street, hit the siren, and floored it. If they didn't clear a path, there might be some bumped bodies. Be purposeful and make a clear statement: ambiguity or hesitation doesn't cut it in this business. People scrambled from my oncoming hurtling vehicle and a few fists struck the sides, accompanied by derisive yells.

Arriving at my destination, I saw a full complement of uniformed, steel-helmeted National Guard troopers, with fixed bayonets on M-1 rifles, preparing to move the rioting crowd from the street. Eager cops grabbed my guns and ammo, grateful for the just-in-time delivery. The troopers moved as a phalanx to disperse the demonstrators, utilizing a well-practiced stomping step—in unison, thrusting bayonet tipped rifles forward in a stabbing motion, all the while chanting, "Move! Move!" with every lunge. Good-bye, rioters.

Open Sesame

Legally sanctioned entries—that is, surreptitious break-ins where the Bureau plants electronic eavesdropping devices and cameras—were a specialty of one brilliant, charismatic FBI Special Agent who worked full time out of Quantico. These kinds of burglaries were often authorized in high-stakes investigations involving organized crime, narcotics, and foreign counterintelligence.

This Agent possessed advanced engineering and technical skills, but midway through his career, he gravitated to criminal burglary/theft activities requiring the same entry skill as his legally sanctioned FBI work. Did he lose his identity as a law enforcer, or did he become addicted to high excitement, thus needing to fuel more and more intense stimulation? Maybe both. While legitimately working for the FBI at Quantico, he conceived and built an electronic device to open electronically controlled garage doors. He called an associate who worked for the CIA in a similar capacity and proposed that they both go out into the northern Virginia suburbs early one morning to test his contraption.

The FBI Agent and the CIA Agent patrolled the Virginia suburbs after three o'clock in the morning trying out the device. His invention, however, worked far too successfully. When our innovative Agent pointed and activated the device at a garage door, it not only opened that door, but it began opening, in sequence, every garage door on the whole block, on both sides. This generated a scene of people running around in their bathrobes, lights going on and off, and general chaos. Upon quick reflection, the two Agents wisely chose to skedaddle before cops arrived.

Shotgun in the Rain

Jerry Traver, a fellow Agent who entered the FBI with me in New Agent Class Number 9, hailed from Kansas. A former Army officer with rapid-fire speech and a quick wit, he was stable, reserved, and seemed a bit isolated. With us for a ride-along one day was a new Agent trainee, a graduate of the University of Mississippi Law School. He was to observe the work Jerry and I did in hopes of gleaning some nuggets of wisdom about how the FBI really works.

The District of Columbia was drenched in an unrelenting, driving rainstorm—not a day to casually cruise about. This was a day to cover leads and look forward to a long, pleasant, morale-building lunch. We headed out to far southeast Washington, near St. Elizabeth's Hospital, the local mental health facility. During the Civil War, Union casualties were treated there, and some were buried on the side of a hill above the Beltway. On Portland Avenue, SE, we visited our favorite family-owned pizza joint, where we relaxed, ordered pizzas and salad, and stuffed ourselves. Satiated from the two-hour lunch, we reluctantly headed back into the rain about 1:50 p.m. I put us in "10-8"—in service (sometimes called "in circus") and available for duty. Immediately, WFO's primary radio dispatcher, Patty, directed our unit to head to far northwest Washington, near the Maryland line in "Code 3 mode"—a highly unusual designation: *Proceed with red light and siren, maximum speed.*

Our destination would be one of DC's many traffic circles. I double-checked our radio assignment, as this entailed a three or four-mile risky run in pelting rain, raising the possibility of a serious crash. She confirmed the directive, from Bank Robbery Supervisor Grant Nana. Somehow, in the entire DC Metropolitan Police Department and FBI, no closer radio unit was available to respond. We were it.

Patty described the emergency. A bank robbery went down in Takoma Park, Maryland, where, while scrambling to escape, three armed robbers had a gun battle with police, then a running skirmish. One robber fired at officers with a shotgun, wounding one of them. They didn't select their escape car very well: all three piled into a stolen Volkswagen—cramped and slow. The fleeing robbers ran afoul of a utility crew on a traffic circle just over the Maryland line in DC, plowed into the Potomac Gas and Electric truck, and turned over. In the heavy rain, the robbers scattered on foot into the adjacent residential neighborhood. We were ordered to conduct a cursory "on-scene" investigation and initiate a search for apprehension.

Siren blaring, illuminated red bubble oscillating on the roof, we sped across the District of Columbia—a very difficult drive. Few streets in the District run parallel or perpendicular, and its four-quadrant layout contains numerous angled streets intersecting traffic roundabouts—inconducive to safe, fast driving. We arrived on scene, rain still pouring down, to find the overturned Volkswagen and the work crew hiding out in their big truck. Alighting from our car, we briefly interviewed the work crew and determined that the three robbers had fled separately in different directions, running down the alley behind the adjacent detached townhouses in this older neighborhood.

We huddled. I looked at the trainee and said, "This is not training school. This is the real deal. If you don't do this one correctly like I tell you, you might get killed—so pay attention. We're going to split up, with each one of us searching an alley where the robbers supposedly ran. Take out your pistol, proceed down the alley slowly, don't miss anything visually, and be ready to shoot. Check under every car and every bush before you proceed, because that's exactly where you're going to find a robber. Search around the shrubbery of each townhouse and check down the rear exterior staircases going into the basements."

Off we went, each of us down a separate alley, with no backup and, as far as we knew, no one en route to help us search for three armed bank robbers, one wielding a shotgun. I started down my alley and did exactly as I had instructed the other two Agents. I found nothing under bushes or parked cars. I looked down the first basement staircase. Nothing. On the grounds of the second townhouse, I checked under the bushes, under the cars, looking up, looking down, and moving slowly, like a stalking cat. Looking over the top of my pistol, I headed for the back of the second townhouse, looked around, and checked under bushes, very, very slowly and gently, for the second time. Peering over the top of the rear staircase—I saw a head.

Bringing my pistol up, I leveled it down the staircase at the suspect, who was seated at the bottom with his back against a concrete retaining wall, his shotgun within reach, propped against a basement door. He looked at me, wet and scared, perhaps still dangerous. I warned, "Don't move, keep your hands in plain view, and don't touch the shotgun, or I'll shoot." I had him stand and pick up the shotgun by the barrel with his left hand, holding it away from his body, and slowly come up the stairs. At the top of the stairs, I took the shotgun from him, put it in a safe place up against the building, got his hands behind his back, and handcuffed him. I then grabbed him by his clothing at the base of the neck, firmly grasped the shotgun by the barrel with my left hand, and marched down the alley toward the circle.

Two Agents pulled up—Cal Ford and Joe Dowling—"heavies" from the C-1 Squad who routinely dealt with kidnappings and bank robberies. Soaked to the skin from the continuing cold rain, I marched the suspect toward the Agents seated in their nice, warm, dry car. I could see the expressions on their faces: "Wow, he got him." The arrest was reminiscent of the armed robber I'd apprehended at the Travelodge in San Francisco. This time around, I applied a lesson from that arrest, where an initial oversight nearly proved fatal: Go slowly, be thorough, look high, look low, and don't miss anything—you might not get a second chance.

Instructing at an FBI Field School in Maui

The FBI Academy at Quantico

13

TICKING TIME BOMBS

Special Agent Kenny Starkes passed me on a stairway landing of the OPO at about 2:30 p.m. one afternoon, saying, "Hey, John, you made it. Just heard your transfer to Quantico's coming through." Smiling, I thanked him for the heads-up. He continued, in a subdued manner, voice dropping, "...and I didn't make it." I let Kenny know I was sorry for his disappointment, reining in my own excitement.

The following morning a sealed envelope came rocketing over my left shoulder, hitting the desk with force enough to scatter papers. Behind me, my supervisor's harsh, hissing voice announced, "I guess you knew this was coming." The creamy-white, high-quality envelope featured a golden Bureau seal, alongside "Office of the Director" in its upper left. Picking it up, I played the moment, slowly opening it for all in the room to see, savoring it a few sweet seconds, eventually saying, "Well, well, well, what have we here? Hmm, I've been transferred to the BSU at Quantico." The BSU was the new Behavioral Science Unit. My performance was met with mild applause (a slow-building clap) and nearly genuine cheers from surrounding Agents.

The Wish List

Years earlier I'd heard about the huge buildup of the "New Academy" from those interesting "training guys" I met at my morning Cuban Coffeehouse ritual. Every ninety days, the Bureau updated the "Dream Sheet," or "Wish List," where every Agent listed his top three "Offices of Preference" (OP). While every Agent expressed his preferred location, it was Bureau policy that all transfers made were solely "for the convenience of the government."

The latest OP update was often a hot topic among veteran Agents over morning coffee. Some guys had worked at the FBI Washington Field Office for fifteen to twenty years, and they weren't going anywhere. I realized I might be destined to become one of these perpetual dreamers, just like the bored police lieutenant in San Francisco going through the motions and reading the orders, if I didn't figure out how to carve out my own destiny.

J. Edgar Hoover established the FBI Police Training School in 1935, during the depths of the Great Depression, in response to fragmented, unfocused American policing. Intelligent, committed local leaders studied ethics, scientific crime detection, investigation, administration, leadership, and organization at the school, which came to be seen as the West Point of law enforcement and garnered the name FBI National Academy (NA).

The National Academy evolved into a cutting-edge, progressive group of collaborative thinker-doers, and a teaching position at Quantico became my goal. I could contribute my Police Wisdom and insight into issues facing officers—I understood their cultural viewpoints, quirks, and idiosyncrasies, allowing me to effectively empathize and communicate with them.

Over copious cups of coffee, Agent Jimmy O'Connor from the FBI Training Division in the OPO told me, "John, to make yourself eligible for a transfer to the NA, you need to get a Masters degree." I subsequently enrolled in the night graduate Criminal Justice program at American University, which emphasized management, sociology, and psychology courses. My thirty units of graduate work in education and California teaching credentials added heft, and I'd authored and taught a patrol procedure course for the SFPD. Added benefit: Instructor positions at Quantico were supervisory level GS-14 with substantially more pay.

Positions at Quantico's campus near the shores of Lake Lunga were highly coveted. I made efforts to strengthen my candidacy, actively letting people at Quantico know that I was very much interested in joining the faculty, finally acknowledging that my education and performance needed to be substantially enhanced by polite, targeted, political effort. My efforts paid off, and in early 1974, I was assigned to a twelve-week "trial-run" position of counselor to the ninety-sixth session at the National Academy.

Finally the BSU

The Behavioral Science Unit was in its formative years, loosely structured and guided with a light, creative hand by Unit Chief Jack Pfaff. Ahead of its time, it resembled a Silicon Valley start-up with its synergistic momentum, offering staffers limitless opportunities to identify and develop innovative programs. I arrived at Quantico (an Agent never arrives on time, but is always about an hour and a half early) with my ever-present spiffy federal briefcase in hand and explored the FBI Academy campus, laid out with buildings accessed via a series of interconnected concrete pathways, which had originally been open. This didn't work weather-wise, so they were now glass enclosed, thereby earning their nickname, "gerbil runs."

My instructions were to report to the Behavioral Science Unit Chief, whose office was located in the Learning Resource Center

(LRC), a centrally located, three-story structure everyone called "The Library." This nickname annoyed LRC Unit Chief Ed Kenney, a pleasant, outgoing ex–NYC cop who earned a master's in Library Science specifically to be reassigned as head of the LRC. Eddie bristled at the limiting moniker "library" because his baby housed cutting-edge (for 1974) electronic access to databases beyond the building—his unit was the first in the FBI to use computers. Kenny made it a top priority to support the operational FBI, handling requests from headquarters and investigative Field Agents, and his able staff addressed a myriad of inquiries, which materially bettered FBI actions worldwide. When the British Foreign Office confronted the Chapeltown race riot in 1975, they asked Eddie if the databases could be queried for relevant articles. "Certainly" was his reply, and the following day two Scotland Yard inspectors arrived at Quantico to personally retrieve the timely background materials.

An elevator took me down to the BSU's "office," located in a basement some twenty feet below ground. Stark, unadorned concrete was the "industrial chic" decorating motif, along with gray steel government furnishings for pizzazz. Sprinklers and pipes jutted out from the ceilings twelve feet above, and lights dangled from chains. The flooring was poured concrete, and gray foundations formed exterior walls, exuding an unfinished, rough strength. I liked the workshop atmosphere. It was as if the Bureau hadn't planned or accounted for the BSU, as no space was available in the main classroom building, where every other academic unit was situated on its ground floor. Our unit seemed orphaned and out-grouped in a basement.

The BSU's castaway status perhaps conveyed a bit of an outlaw, somewhat disruptive image. Maybe it wasn't quite ready for "prime time" acceptance—it had a blush of taint, with all that radical, squishy, unproven "behavioral" stuff. Perhaps we weren't quite as washed as the established, "legitimate" legal, education, and management units. Everything was gray but the atmosphere. Eager enthusiasm and electricity permeated the air. You wanted to get on board. The whole package was contagious.

The BSU responsibilities were four pronged: (1) Teach courses for police managers attending the FBI's twelve-week National Academy course; (2) Instruct new Agent trainees and veteran Agents "in-service" classes; (3) Conduct regional Field Training Schools for police and sheriff departments; (4) Conduct research.

I walked into Unit Chief Jack Pfaff's office, expecting the normal "new-guy" greeting. He immediately gave me marching orders. "Go upstairs—you'll be sitting in on Liebman and Schwartz's Crisis Intervention (CI) weeklong seminar. I want you to closely monitor their presentation, work with them, and be ready to write and create our version of how police should handle disputes more safely and efficiently." This wasn't about big, splashy encounters—it was dangerous bread-and-butter, everyday policing, which traditionally received no attention.

Life-Saving Research

"Domestics" were the most common call for police, often fraught with unpredictability, pent-up emotion, and danger. Frequent players in CI incidents included people under the influence of drugs or alcohol and the mentally unstable. Officers were at risk of injury, or worse, when handling these potentially violent, explosive cases. There was a lot to learn. I'd have to hit the ground in a full sprint.

Many police confronting domestics were untrained and attempted to resolve conflicts by offering commonsense advice, ordering one party to "take a hike to cool off" or making an arrest. These techniques sometimes worked in the short-term—however, lack of resolution or a hopeful pathway forward assured continued long-term deterioration of the problem, and repeated calls involving the same actors. As underlying problems remained unaddressed, this merry-go-round worsened and intensified with time, devouring police resources and increasing danger for everyone.

In the early 1970s, psychologists Ron Liebman and Jeffrey Schwartz did a superb job of researching the Crisis Intervention field, working with local police to develop a disciplined, step-by-step approach that enhanced safety and efficiency for all participants in these volatile situations. I worked with Liebman and Schwartz and drew on their expertise in building a staged, sequential CI model response strategy. Our program utilized seven major principles, each with specific techniques for patrol officers to employ in explosive disputes:

1. Initial assessment, or "seeing the scene"
2. Safety for participants, defusing/calming
3. Securing information and interviewing
4. Selecting and employing a dispute- or life-appropriate resolution strategy, picked from a menu of options, including:
5. Mediating an agreement
6. Referral to a social service agency
7. Arrest—as a last resort

While the principles were distinct, application in the working environment allowed for fuzzy overlap. In September 1974 we held our first three-and-a-half-day regional Crisis Intervention Field School with the Toledo, Ohio, Police Department. Over the ensuing three years, we took our CI show on the road across the United States, delivering more than fifty intensive three- and four-day regional courses. Our research, course building, and teaching reinforced the Bureau's pioneering role and continued commitment to improving policing and better serving officers.

My CI partner, Dick Harper, and I were curious about the circumstances in which police officers were killed while handling dispute calls. We spent many evenings in our cellar digs culling, sorting, evaluating, and discussing the Bureau's "Uniformed Crime Report," which included narratives of individual officer encounters culminating in casualties. A glaring, heretofore unrecognized problem area leapt out from the data: cops being killed with their own guns. We emphasized to students, "In every dispute an officer addresses, there is a gun involved." Students would initially respond with blank stares, murmurs of "No way," and shaking heads. Police never saw themselves as carrying the potential tool of their own demise, yet 20–25 percent of officers killed in altercations were shot and killed with their own gun—dropped, wrestled from a hand, or ripped from its holster.

The Lone Star

Attempting to quell a domestic dispute, an Austin police officer inadvertently shot a sixteen-year-old boy in front of his father. The community responded loudly and vocally. Police were rocked by press criticism of their apparently inept tactics, and tensions ran high. In the aftermath, the BSU received an urgent request in September 1975 from the Austin Police Department. Bob Ressler and I, as experts (the guys from out of town with suitcases), would train officers in the latest crisis-management concepts and techniques at the University of Texas Law School.

Walking to our first scheduled class, we were joined by some officers and Crispin James, a reporter for the *Austin-American Statesman* newspaper. She sat in on many of our classes and wrote a series of articles headlined: "Home Squabbles Tough on Police, FBI Explains," "Policemen Learn New Job Skills," "Policemen Instructed on Psychopath Danger," and "Policemen Must Know How to Handle Psychopaths." Crispin's article, "Police to Train APD Comrades," detailed how three Austin police officers who were attending the course— Lt. Jerry Culp, Sgt. Jerry Spain, and Officer Vernon Magness—would take the information learned and conduct in-service training schools for other Austin police officers on methods of handling family disturbances. This procedure of "planting the seeds" for local departments to nourish the concept, strategy, and techniques was repeated in cities across the country.

Toward the end of the course, James interviewed me about other critical issues in policing. Thinking of the trauma faced by the very officers I was there to teach, I asked her rhetorically, "What about the crises police themselves experience?" Extrapolating, I continued on this thought, explaining how the pressures of policing negatively impact officers' interactions with their families, in turn affecting their attitudes at work (especially responding to "domestics"), activating and reinforcing a self-perpetuating cycle where some officers become "ticking time bombs," ineffective at work, perhaps even dangerous, and malcontents at home. James subsequently wrote "Policemen 'Time Bombs' Worry FBI Instructor." These interviews and her articles served as a nascent blueprint for future explorations.

Police work, defined and driven by external cues, is rife with physical and verbal exchanges occurring in a crunched, compressed environment of time constraints. Officers must handle the current assignment, or "run," and get on to the next call, without deep pondering or reflection and absent responsibility for mid- to long-term resolution or ultimate workable outcome. Cop culture, emphasizing and reinforcing reflexive, repetitive reactions, operates within rigid boundaries in an emotionally detached military/warrior mode: contemplation, thoughtfulness, and humanistic orientation erode and succumb. Decisions boil down to, "We've always done it this way," or "My Sergeant said…"

Shallow approaches and techniques for quick, "successful" conflict abatement inculcate over time, breeding mindsets of superficial confidence with increasingly authoritarian overtones. Officers can become isolated, by degrees, in a lifestyle cocoon where the professional and personal intermingle, gradually generating an extreme, even dictatorial outlook. The officer-husband-father devolves into interrogator-boss-expert, nullifying open interactions.

"Talking crisis" rekindled my interest in the dark, underacknowledged side of policing, spurring me to later create a course entitled Police Stress and Personal Problems, exploring a topic historically swept under the rug. Classic denial dictated: "Guardians cannot have flaws."

Policemen 'time bombs' worry FBI instructor

10-13-75

By CRISPIN JAMES
Staff Writer

During 15 months of teaching, FBI National Academy instructor John Minderman has lent an ear to police officers from 700 to 800 police departments across the nation.

These candid conversations — often gleaned from coffee breaks between police seminar sessions — have convinced Minderman there are "innumerable walking wounded" in the nation's police departments.

He is also convinced police administrators have lit fuses on officer "time bombs."

He says the "time bombs" are fused when administrators insist on better educated policemen yet fail to address the career, psychological and social needs of their officers.

Minderman says the "time bombs" are exploding into police strikes and are short circuiting the careers of idealistic men who become "burn outs" when they realize they are not crime fighters but "garbage" collectors of social ills they can't cure.

Minderman, in Austin last week to conduct a crisis training school for Austin police officers, was once a self-styled "Super Cop" who experienced "burn out" as a San Francisco policeman.

Within several months, he says he will begin his own research into the psychological needs of police officers. He plans to develop an FBI training package on police problems for administrators and officers who attend sessions at the FBI academy in Quantico, Va.

Minderman was one of two FBI agents first assigned to investigate the burglary of Democratic National Headquarters in Washington's Watergate building.

But his career as an FBI agent began only after he spent several years marking time — a frustrated, disillusioned policeman.

Born in San Francisco, Minderman's first ambition was to be a television or radio news commentator. But his father discouraged him — labeling the news business "not a profession."

Minderman succumbed to his father's pressure, obtained a degree in social science and a secondary teaching degree.

He never taught. He joined the San Francisco Police Department and received patrol assignment in the same district of his birth.

Earning the reputation of a "super patrolman" for aggressiveness on his beat, Minderman was commended for outstanding performance of duty 44 times and was awarded five meritorious citations during his eight years in the department.

He was once cited for rescuing several elderly persons trapped by a raging fire in a hotel.

When he failed to be promoted to the department's detective bureau, he became bitter and his frustration "burned out" his career.

He lost all incentive and joined the traffic bureau, a daytime job requiring little but accident investigation.

Fellow officers didn't help.

"I got nothing but sympathy from them," he said.

His realized he should leave the department. Minderman resigned, became an FBI special agent and served in the Dallas and Washington field offices before assignment in the behavioral sciences section of the academy in Quantico.

While in Washington — and investigating Watergate — Minderman earned a masters degree in administration of justice at American University.

But his early career as a burned out patrolman made him empathetic to problems of police officers.

Minderman says the social isolation felt by many officers and related problems of alcoholism, divorce and suicide have never been acknowledged by police administrators.

"If you look at priorities reflected in police academies you get a clear view of how police administrators identify priorities," he said. "They have many hours blocked for report writing, firearm handling and department policy. Instead of emphasis on the mechanical aspects of the job there needs to be more emphasis on the officer's psychological and social needs."

He said policemen are in constant contact with the sick, wounded and distraught.

Since officers cannot psychologically "share the pain" with all persons they meet, they build a defense mechanism called "isolation from affect."

Unfortunately, the isolation often permeates the officer's personal life as well, causing conflicts in his own family.

JOHN MINDERMAN
FBI instructor

Another problem, according to Minderman, is that although officers are pushed to get college degrees, their jobs are not restructured to give them more responsibility and decision-making powers in the department.

"What you do is create more educated, sophisticated, demanding, questioning police officers," said Minderman. "Police officers 30 years and younger tend to be more militant anyway. With the added enlightenment of greater education, the chance for more militant police officers is increasing as time goes by."

(source: The Austin American Statesman)

10-11-75

Policemen learn new job skills

By CRISPIN JAMES
Staff Writer

A new language and a greater perception of the subtle skills needed to deflate citizen squabbles followed 23 policemen out the door Friday at the end of a week-long FBI "crisis intervention" school.

Sharing such new-found concepts as "defuse," "body space," "mediation" and "brief interview," the officers laid plans to present training in crisis intervention to 440 fellow officers.

Offering a round of applause to FBI instructor John Minderman, the officers set Dec. 8 as the date for the first in-service training school to begin. All officers of the department will receive 16 hours of instruction in crisis intervention during a 24-week period.

The 22 city policemen and one University of Texas policeman were told this week their attitudes at the scene of a disturbance can determine the mood of a crisis.

Since family disturbances ranked as the No. 1 killer of policemen in the United States in 1973 and 1974, officer skills are vital for his safety — and the citizen's, Minderman said.

"We've all had to use these skills at one time or another, but this is the first time we've seen all those skills brought together in an organized manner for us to look at," Lt. Jerry Cuip commented.

Minderman told the officers — a cross-section of supervisors and patrolmen — that they should not impose their value systems on complainants, but instead should elicit all sides of the issue and let the complainants make a decision.

He said if possible, officers should make more use of community social service agencies for referral of persons with chronic alcohol, marriage, drug or mental problems.

Minderman emphasized that repeated police visits to the same address waste time which could be used for preventive crime patrol and increase the possibility of injury or death to citizens and police.

This October marks one year since police shot to death an East Austin citizen during such a confrontation — the catalyst which prompted police supervisors to request the FBI crisis school.

"The problem is, policemen really don't have any business being at most family disturbances," Capt. Royal Wilson said. "He goes in as a third person, walks inside a home where no laws have been broken and finds that the hostilities are transferred to him."

The fact that policemen are available at all hours, seven days a week, when most social service agencies close at 5 p.m., make policemen the "instrument for public security," Minderman said.

For two days, the policemen became actors, portraying drunks and irate husbands and citizens in skits designed to test mediation skills of those assigned to be "officers."

The skits were videotaped and critiqued and will be used to instruct others on the force.

NOW, C'MON, FOLKS—
LET'S WORK THIS OUT
LIKE RATIONAL ADULTS—
OKAY?

Setting the Course

My colleague Howard "Bud" Teton and I coauthored an article for the January 1977 edition of the *FBI Monthly Journal—Law Enforcement Bulletin* titled "Police Personal Problems—Practical Considerations for

Administrators." We outlined a collaborative approach, which centered on defining under-acknowledged issues, proposing engagement, and exploring pathways toward embracing solutions.

The Police Stress Conference became a reality at Quantico in mid-January 1977. I cobbled together a three-and-a-half-day seminar, featuring presentations by psychologists who were employed by policing agencies. Established police-stress experts came together to deliver a comprehensive overview of the existing knowledge, programs, and techniques applicable to reducing stress-related problems in policing agencies. Presenters included PhDs John Stratton (LA Sheriff's Office); John Berberich (Seattle PD); Illana Hadar, Susan Saxe, and Martin Raiser (LAPD); Mike Roberts (San Jose PD); and police officials Joseph Barry, Ed Donovan, and Joe Ravine (Boston PD); and Inspector Richard Caretti (Detroit PD). This symposium established a groundbreaking national network and feedback-exchange loop of subject-matter experts and police contacts.

Our success in opening up discussion of this issue allowed me to construct a three-unit course accredited by the University of Virginia entitled Police Stress Recognition and Personal Problems. The easy part was putting the course together. More challenging was presenting the material to ranking police officers in an unthreatening way. Police project strength and control. How could society's authority figures admit to perceived weakness and seek help? It was a tightrope without a net. Our classroom had to be a confidential, secure, neutral zone, a kind of sealed-away, secret retreat. Topical presentations generated free-flowing, informal discussions, which occasionally evolved into group therapy. The course laid out the issues in an objective way, casual but structured. Illustrative examples could never directly refer to classroom students, unless a posed question sparked a discussion.

At the heart of key stress-related issues are basic, defining, framing questions: What is stress? What effects does stress have on police officers? We defined "stress" as "the rate of wear and tear on the body and the mind," and "distress" as a state wherein the body and mind become increasingly unable to cope, deal, or adjust to the rate, frequency, or intensity of wear and tear, eventually deteriorating into gradual erosion of flexibility and capability. We focused on emotional stress, which occurs when we become agitated, depressed, or challenged to our limits, struggling to find a coping mechanism. If prolonged and allowed to accumulate, it becomes problematic, evolving into "acute distress." The cumulative effect of many pressures faced by law enforcement officers can exasperate personal and professional problems, thereby increasing personal pressures to a crisis point, activating inappropriate responses and even breakdown.

John Wayne Syndrome

Excessive stress or distress begets predictable patterns of behavior that specifically target police officers. One prominent behavioral straitjacket that police commonly acquire is the "John Wayne syndrome"—a hypermacho cluster of attitudes and actions. Officers begin experiencing feelings of invincibility and simultaneously build an emotional wall of denial to any degree of perceived or actual threat. The emerging constellation of language, attitudes, and actions that impacted officers exhibit can be so over-the-top it's borderline comical. When burgeoning overconfidence overrides, even blinds, reality, the impact has devastating consequences for officers' personal lives and breeds dangerous professional limitations, especially in the area of safety. It can be deflating and destabilizing for an officer to hear the John Wayne syndrome cluster of attributes and symptoms described, even in an impersonal, clinical manner, as it may cause creeping personal doubt and self-awareness.

When I conducted a hostage negotiation school with Bud Teton at a Holiday Inn in Torrance, California, many of the attending officers were SWAT trained. I pointed out that an officer in the grip of John Wayne syndrome might be unable to reach down and plumb the depths of his humanity to build and establish the trust so necessary to negotiate with a hostage-taker. As I graphically and dramatically described the manifestations and impact of the syndrome, the class grew noticeably uneasy, especially one attendee.

Following our morning session, we lunched together absent the fidgety officer. The afternoon session was twenty minutes gone when a scantily clad cocktail waitress knocked and entered the classroom, holding a tray with three drinks. Class stopped. She asked, by name, for the fidgeting officer—he answered up and paid for the drinks. No one uttered a word, and class resumed. He quickly consumed the beverages, and after the next break, he disappeared, never to return. Confronting the reality of this syndrome had put this officer well beyond his coping tolerance. Was the straitjacket too tight?

Unique Stressors

It was crucial we build a collegial atmosphere where students continuously felt comfortable, knowing they weren't being judged. Sensitive problems like alcoholism and family difficulties were explored in our course in an intensive, self-revealing process. The course concluded with students writing a research paper detailing an actual stressful incident (factual with fictional names), identifying the stressors, proposing a positive manner to handle the situation, and offering preventative strategies. Confronting and admitting vulnerability, minus the big blue shield, tore down the protective facade of denial; fostered self-knowledge, insight, and growth; and was ultimately liberating.

Law enforcement is not, of course, the only field affected by pressure and stress factors. However, police work is among the highest-stress occupations. Police are never fully "off duty." Many carry their weapons constantly and thus are ever vigilant for threat. Their actions are subject to being second-guessed, filmed, and judged—administratively, legally, and publicly. This constant, intense scrutiny produces not just constant vigilance, but can cause hypervigilance, a state of suspicion, wariness, and mistrust that's wearingly corrosive and doesn't permit normal relaxation—so vital for physical rest and emotional rejuvenation. Officers can lose their sensitivity, flexibility, and objectivity, thereby becoming less suited to deal with all aspects of their lives.

Divisive Forces

Individual law officers' personalities and personal lives are only part of the picture when police stress is analyzed. Police culture also fuels and feeds on attitudes that heighten stress risk. Isolated by odd hours, and reliance on backup begins to shift the enforcers' role—officers can fall victim to "groupthink," wherein questions generate "obvious" answers, which become reinforced and entrenched by subtle, ever-present pressures to conform to rigid group values.

Sociologist William H. Whyte coined the term "groupthink," which "conceptualizes the mechanism by which tightly knit groups, cut off from outside influence, rapidly converge on normatively 'correct' positions, becoming … institutionally impervious to criticism, indifferent to out-group opposition, adverse to in-group dissent, and ever more confident of their own unimpeachable rectitude." [quoted in Kevin Dutton: *The Wisdom of Psychopaths*]

With police culture and organizational structure so rigidly defined, deviance from group norms is questioned, even seen as a threat or a failing. Flaws and skewed perceptions are denied as flowing from a police-working environment. Psychologist Irving Janis [also quoted in *The Wisdom of Psychopaths*] noted: "Humans can be paralyzed by a code of conduct: an all-consuming requirement to toe the party line." Survival reliance on other officers (backup) breeds obligatory dependence as isolated officers become increasingly enveloped in an inflexible cocoon.

Police culture selectively identifies actions that enhance its warrior self-image, while scandal, corruption, and individual acts connoting legal or moral difficulties are seen as isolated aberrations, "one-offs," or the acts of mavericks. In *Trying Not to Try: The Art and Science of Spontaneity,* Edward Singerland writes, "Still grounded as a basic feature of Western thought is *extreme individualism.* The ideal person in Western philosophy is not only disembodied but also *radically alone.* For the past couple hundred years in the West, the dominant view of human nature had been that we are all pursuing our own self-interest."

The culture itself is seldom considered a catalyst or an endemic source of problems. This "pass" causes an absence of needed illuminating introspection and self-reflection, and problems become deep rooted. Virtues such as togetherness, unity and "police family" are extolled and expressed in ritualistic bonding gatherings. This dual process—blind-eyeing entrenched problems while unifying the group via solidarity rituals and ceremonies—slows progress, further isolating police as a homogenous culture, distanced from the public, rather than defining officers as independent individual professionals.

I'd rubbed up against the dark side of policing as a working officer in a department that was born during the California Gold Rush of the 1850s. Residual pockets and isolated incidents of illegalities had long been a part of life in "The City," and by extension, why would one expect society's key local law enforcement agency to be excluded from this sly, wink-wink, juiced process? My eight-and-a-half-year tenure in the 1960s provided an intimate view of the many personal and organizational problems police encounter. Ethical challenges imbued the normal, routine policing performed by any officer and bestowed me valuable lessons and insights I'd later apply investigating the twisted conspiracies and improprieties of Watergate.

Medicine for Modern Times

When the *Great British Psychopath Survey* recently "assessed the prevalence of psychopathic traits within the national workforce," police officer was rated at number seven. Ex-FBI Agents involved in planning and executing burglaries? The highest FBI official anointing himself patriotic serial leaker and coolly deflecting blame? A cluster of CIA types subverting, undermining the American political process by actively committing multiple felonies on American soil? Peel back the layers to examine the behavioral characteristics that seem to define these men.

In *Untangling the Mind,* Psychiatrist D. Theodore George observes, "The most distinctive quality of psychopaths is the lack of empathy... [t]hey have no visceral feelings about others and are incapable of understanding other people's perspectives...many ruthless, ambitious people have mild versions of some psychopathic traits...[t]here are degrees of appropriate and inappropriate predatory behavior. In people with socially accepted psychopathic traits, the 'button' for lacking emotion and predatory behavior is pushed intermittently and mildly. Perhaps they feel a business situation demands manipulating coworkers." He called such people "The Everyday Psychopath." In *Snakes in Suits*, Hare and Babiak found that "not all psychopaths are in prison—some are in business and the boardroom." They termed such individuals "functional psychopaths."

In *The Wisdom of Psychopaths*, Kevin Dutton insightfully proposes, "Who wouldn't benefit at certain points in their lives from kicking one or two 'psychopathic traits' up a notch?"

Dutton identified "seven core principles of psychopathy that—apportioned judiciously and applied with due care and attention—can help us get exactly what we want, can help us respond, rather than react, to the challenges of modern-day living, can transform our outlook from victim to victor—without turning into a villain: "(1) Ruthlessness (2) Charm (3) Focus (4) Mental Toughness (5) Fearlessness (6) Mindfulness (7) Action."

"The power of the skill set lay squarely in its application. Certain situations would call for more of some traits than others. The secret, unquestionably, was context. It wasn't about being a psychopath—it was rather about being a method psychopath. About being able to step into character when the situation demanded it. But then, when the exigency had passed, to revert to one's normal persona."

A brilliant attorney once commented to Dr. Dutton, "Psychopathy (if that's what you want to call it) is like medicine for modern times. If you take it in moderation, it can prove extremely beneficial."

In *The Psychopath Inside*, Dr. James Fallon, a neuroscientist and medical school professor, confesses he considers himself "a normal guy," although his colleagues frequently termed him "a sociopath," citing the following behavioral characteristics: "manipulative, charming but devious, an intellectual bully, completely lacking scruples, cunning liar, living by a selective moral code, irresponsible, completely unfeeling, cold, unempathetic, emotionally shallow, 'The Great I AM,' pathological liar, blame others, completely overblown sense of self-importance, looking for a buzz, a need for constant stimulation, fearless, irresponsibly puts others at great risk with yourself, very popular but with many shallow relationships, and no sense of guilt whatsoever."

Dr. Fallon concluded: "What everyone seemed to be telling me was that I was 'Psychopath Lite,' or a prosocial psychopath, someone who has many of the traits of psychopathy, other than the violent criminality and antisocial tendencies, a type of psychopathy in which one finds socially acceptable outlets for one's aggression and which is manifested in a cold, narcissistic manipulation of people."

Profiles in Criminology

One of the brilliant "entry" guys—an Agent who worked out of Quantico with expertise defeating locked entries into buildings (and much more)—was fond of saying, "Whatever man can do, man can undo." Circumventing security systems or picking challenging locks, he worked "back to front" through deduction, applying what he knew to "unlock" what he didn't know. In effect, he was reverse engineering, mirroring the approach developed and utilized in behavioral profiling.

How do you discover a profile? Begin with the assumption that each movement, act, or operation a person performs or omits is an attempt to satisfy some desire or requirement. There's a reason, logical or illogical, known or unknown, for each human action or lack thereof—thus an underlying behavioral profile, or lifestyle map, exists dormant, quiescent, waiting to be discovered, deciphered, and fleshed out.

Quantico's Behavioral Science Unit (BSU) developed and incubated the now-established professional field of criminal profiling by engaging with police to develop the first systematic evaluation and cataloguing of rough-cut "criminal personality" sketches. Agents Bud Teton and Pat Mullaney did the groundbreaking work with Bob Ressler, who actually coined the phrase "serial murderer" as he brought this field into full flower. John Douglas added his substantial talents, becoming the dean and superstar of the field.

A key factor in the development of profiling was the collaboration of Quantico instructors with the police officers in the NA classroom. Instructors took the theoretical and interpretive aspects of criminal behavioral psychology and sociology, established as traits, or "emerging trends and patterns," then selected and applied these findings and insights to particular cases and homicide crime scenes, eventually crafting a theoretical "best guess" criminal portrait, or profile.

Information from investigations supplemented a behavioral narrative, and from this process, new insights and approaches flowed out of the classroom. These were stored, catalogued, and applied to actual pending cases, gradually building and continuously refining our knowledge base. It was a constant process of add-subtract-modify and asking ourselves, "How could these insights, ideas, and concepts be applied to new cases?"

In 1888, Sir Arthur Conan Doyle's immensely successful fictional detective Sherlock Holmes capitalized on the author's medical training and background to imbue his character with medical-type diagnostic skills, applied logically through deductive analysis and reasoning to homicide investigations, among others. "Profiling" certainly wasn't invented by the FBI's BSU at Quantico; it was refined and enhanced by knowledgeable, insightful FBI Instructor Special Agents. Progressive, inquisitive National Academy police students brought difficult cases to their sessions, and this collaboration fueled our efforts in defining, refining, and expanding this emerging field.

Successes begat confidence, and soon our unit's personnel were fielding calls from police detectives nationwide, requesting help on unsolved murders. Police–FBI collaborative exchanges led to the conception and launch of Quantico's Profiling Research Project. Collaboration, breakthroughs, insights, multiple feedback loops, forthright criticism, dialogues, and debate produced psychological profiles to help officers solve crimes by identifying, dissecting, and analyzing behavioral patterns. Criminal profiling soon became an accepted, prominent part of law enforcement worldwide because it worked.

Think Fast Act Faster

Recently published behavioral and scientific researched findings validate many theory-based tactical responses we advocated at Quantico's

BSU. These newly defined concepts identify behavioral patterns and provide a better understanding of human actions within quick-paced, contentious, threatening, adversarial engagements by examining mental process-engagement and discretionary decision-making, and is widely applicable to athletes, first responders, military combatants, and others.

In his acclaimed new book *Head Strong,* Michael D. Matthews, former deputy sheriff and current Professor of Engineering Psychology at West Point, writes "the importance of and ability to make fast and accurate decisions is critical, fundamental to operational success in war. Hesitation compromises the ability to respond to the target." Fast and accurate decision-making requires "Situational awareness ... a cognitive attribute critical for making rapid and accurate decisions under stressful conditions with limited decision-making time. It represents the ability of a person to size up a situation and act in ways that maximize the chances of success and minimize the chances of failure or harm." Matthews spells out "in its barest form" his version of this reciprocal, evaluative-decision-action looping process:

(1) Accurately perceive the situation in which they find themselves,

(2) Understand what the perceived information means and

(3) Project what is likely to happen next."

In policing, as in life, timing is critical. Gut feelings guide crucial decisions in rapidly evolving situations, where speed and accuracy dynamically combine to delineate a path to ultimate "success." On the evening of June 16, 1972, first responding police and FBI Agents began applying this principle of "Situational Awareness," as we embarked on an epic scramble to embrace a moving front. Our scrappy C-2 Squad prevailed by thinking fast and acting faster.

John with Attorney General Edward Meese and George Jarvis

John with SAC Richard Held

14

RETURN OF THE NATIVE

Across the Pond

Today's FBI circles the world with a significant presence, collaborating with foreign partners. In my era, its foreign role was more limited. Selected FBI Agents filled posts in our foreign embassies under the title "Legal Attaché" (LA—possessing a distinctive, diplomatic ring), building and nurturing bridges with agencies and foreign services. LAs collaborated through Headquarters with all US law enforcement agencies, arranging and facilitating the coverage and handling of critically needed inquiries by foreign, cooperating police. Many felons who'd "flown the coop" were located and returned to local US jurisdictions due to their dedicated efforts.

In 1978, I represented the FBI's Training Division as the initial "Exchange Instructor in Residence" at the British National Police College. Located in the bucolic southern English countryside, historic Bramshill House—one of the largest Jacobean mansions in England—was built in the early seventeenth century and influenced by the Italian Renaissance. The high-ceilinged, three-story, brick structure was host in the 1820s to top-level cricket matches, and its ample grounds featured a lake that provided peaceful surroundings where students and instructors could clear the cobwebs by taking meandering rowboat rides amid cruising swans—in stark contrast to gritty, high-intensity street policing.

Bramshill House has been the British police staff college since 1960. The institution evolved with the timely police issues of particular eras and it is currently tasked with "working with police around the world to improve global security." My six-month residency focused on direct exposure to field policing and immersion in selected classes at the college. Many policing approaches adopted in America emanated from what the British originally conceived and built. Their first formal police force was formed in 1829 with the "Peelers," or "Bobbies," nicknamed for then–Home Secretary (later Prime Minister) Sir Robert Peel. I'd always admired the reserved, quietly confident "on watch presence" approach of British police officers. Their quiet style seemed highly effective in "mirroring" desired public behavior: calmed and understated, geared to defuse flaring tempers and hostility via this modeling example.

I toured most of the twenty-seven police regions and was treated to marvelous countryside and seaside vistas in the company of local officials who briefed me on their forces' policing approaches. My drivers were "specialist officers" who'd undergone six months of pursuit and high-performance training, and would often modestly show off their precision driving prowess on sharp curves of hilly countryside.

British cops weren't afraid to "stick it to the Yanks." One of my Detective Inspector contacts set up a meeting at a location in London. I walked about, attempting to follow, but occasionally deviating from, his seemingly straightforward directions. Eventually I wound up at the designated site. A veteran undercover officer in prior years, he delighted in regaling me with how he deduced where I might be "turned around a bit" while trying to locate our meeting site. He'd actually "picked me up" several blocks away and followed me undetected while I struggled to find the site. Chalk one up for the Brits. We had a laugh over beers in a nearby pub.

Hot topics in the classroom included labor issues, the emergence of unions, and how to deal with worker associations. Relying on the work and insights of two Quantico instructors, Larry Monroe and Dick Ayers, I pitched in as point man to provide an American perspective, information, and trends, as unions had been thoroughly studied and researched at Quantico. US chiefs—having passed through the "confrontational fight 'em" phase—were learning and beginning to apply "get ahead of the curve philosophy" techniques to increase positive engagement and negotiation to resolution. When I presented Crisis Intervention and Police Stress seminars, they generated engaging discussions. My on-scene efforts with British academic colleagues seemed fruitful. A couple of weekends, I went home with a British instructor and lived with his family. It was an altogether wonderful experience where I hoped I'd made some contribution to bettering international policing relations.

Adjustments on the Fly

Back in the States, en route to teach an FBI Police Stress Field School course in Fort Smith, Arkansas, another Agent and I ran through the Memphis airport desperately trying to make a 6:30 p.m. Friday flight on Republic Airlines. Totally out of breath, we stopped at the boarding check-in counter. As we dutifully presented our FBI identification to the counter agent and signed a form authorizing our carrying firearms on board, he mentioned, "You guys may have a problem with this captain." Translation: "will have."

We went down a ramp to the Convair 550 turboprop and entered a full cabin, taking the last two seats. About five minutes later, while we were still on the ground, a smiling captain emerged from the cockpit and proceeded toward us. He leaned over. "Are you the FBI Agents?" I stated that we were. "Are you armed?" Again I replied in the affirmative.

With a whiff of attitude, he informed us, "You have to surrender your bullets or firearms. I have a policy of not allowing anybody to fly behind me armed." This, pardon the pun, was not going to fly with me. The FBI is always armed. Go ahead—make my day.

I pointed out, "We can't do that because we're required to fly armed. If we gave you our bullets, we'd merely have pieces of inert steel in our holsters." The law and established policy were clearly on our side, yet this dispute quickly developed into a standoff, with the captain finally issuing an ultimatum that the aircraft wasn't moving until we disarmed to his satisfaction. My final statement to him: "You may not fly this plane, but somebody will." A sour expression engulfed his face as he bolted for the cockpit.

Following our verbal standoff, we sat in our seats for the next fifteen minutes as other passengers began acting annoyed, a few throwing dirty looks. Nowadays people pay a bit more respect to federal marshals flying our airways armed, putting their own lives at risk to protect others from ever-present, lurking danger. At last, a deflated-looking captain emerged from the cockpit, businesslike and very serious. He leaned over and told us that he was going to make an exception, just this one time. My fellow Agent, who had expressed some mild concern about my handling of the situation, asked me what I thought had happened that caused the pilot to cave. I explained, "The pilot probably called his wife. She analyzed the situation and advised him that he best fly the plane right now and forget about the FBI Agents. 'We've got house payments and two kids in college. Just do your job, honey.'"

Headed Home

Three years into teaching the Police Stress course at Quantico and across the country, I explored various university PhD programs. My limited, haphazard inquiry was discouraging, as I couldn't find a suitable fit. The Bureau then instituted a new program allowing qualified supervisors at HQ to transfer as Field Supervisors to a city of their choice when a vacancy occurred. I decided to take a chance, undergo an "interesting" three-day evaluation process, and become eligible for another challenging aspect of the FBI.

When given a choice between San Francisco and Los Angeles, I gave a great deal of thought to LA, very aware of that office's excellent reputation. At a gathering at Quantico of SACs, the San Francisco SAC, Bill Neuman, engaged me in a long conversation and encouraged me to take SF, as he thought I was a good fit. That sealed the deal—I was headed home.

When I left Quantico, I needed to find someone to continue the Police Stress Program. James (Jim) Reese, who was awarded a Bronze Star in Vietnam, seemed the best candidate: intelligent, serious, and an excellent presenter, with witty, biting humor. He was hesitant to take over, initially declining the opportunity and proposal I offered. I pressed him, emphasizing the potential growth of the field and relevance of stress and personal problems as every issue in policing ultimately touched this area. Eventually, Jim took the Police Stress Program and raised it to new levels. After retiring from the FBI, he formed his own consultancy and went on to become a bestselling author and internationally known motivational and keynote speaker.

In early 1981, I packed my little yellow Honda to the hilt and head-ed west to San Francisco. Some thirteen years earlier, I'd left to pursue a Bureau career, now I was headed back in the 1980s as a designated FBI Field Supervisor. Over the next eight years, I would be responsible for diverse squads including: Organized Crime/Narcotics, Bank Robbery/ Kidnapping, Fugitives/Applicants, and Counterterrorism.

Driving cross-country, I reflected on my decisions. Was it wise to leave my established Quantico position? Should I have opted for sunny LA? What might lie ahead in the next episodes on the streets of San Francisco? Arriving in the Bay Area, I walked along Ocean Beach in-haling the cool refreshing salt air, realizing how much I'd missed "The City," my family, friends, and sourdough bread.

✵ ✵ ✵

Go Army

The Presidio, a historic army base founded in 1776 as the Spanish empire's northernmost military outpost, sits atop a rocky hunk of San Francisco. It anchors the south abutment of the Golden Gate Bridge, bordered by San Francisco Bay on the north, its westerly limits em-bracing spectacular cliffs overlooking blue-green surf, and is heavily crisscrossed by public roads and intermittent eucalyptus tree groves, with natives and tourists as common as army personnel. Any felony committed on its rolling landscape was by default a Bureau case. Given its unhindered public access, with city residential neighborhoods on its southern and eastern edges, Agents worked many "crimes on a govern-ment reservation" on Presidio grounds.

I hadn't met the current commanding officer and was pleasantly surprised when Col. Gene Hawkins introduced himself via a phone call.

We shared common roots as native San Franciscans and fondly talked about "The City." He invited me to a staff conference to discuss an upcoming protest demonstration, which he viewed as quite problematic. Could the FBI possibly help? "Why, sure" was always my answer. I don't recall ever turning down a request for help. "Helping" was always a way to mitigate, if even in a small way, someone else's difficulty. Many Agents of my era were military veterans and the Bureau fully supported our nation's fighting forces.

I looked forward to meeting Colonel Hawkins and was curious to hear his concerns about the impending demonstration. Driving into the Presidio on a clear, warm spring day, I savored the park-like ambience. I walked to an administration building near the parade grounds and proceeded to a conference room on the second floor. No curtains or adornments trimmed the windows of the square room, which was furnished with utilitarian tables and precisely aligned, straight-backed, stainless steel chairs.

Hawkins and his officers faced the challenge of a large demonstration of animal-rights protesters who were targeting an army intelligence and research facility, which allegedly used animals in experiments aimed at improving treatment of soldiers' war wounds. The facility bordered a high-volume public auto throughway that provided primary access from downtown San Francisco to the Golden Gate Bridge. The facility could not have been in a worse location to isolate and contain an angry protest. As an Agent in Washington, DC, I played an undercover role infiltrating night demonstrations at Dupont Circle in the 1970s. That could get very dicey, as the uniformed metro police did not know my identity. Years after my initial demo exposure, plus training and experience as a Quantico hostage negotiation instructor, I was back in my hometown applying this knowledge in a high-stakes, roll-of-the-dice confrontation.

I listened while Hawkins and about ten staff officers pondered their information. Possible responses centered on maintaining control by using combat Military Police (MPs). Hanging over the entire discussion—the unspoken dictum that the Army could never be seen as losing control—Army strategies and operational tactics were geared for foreign combat zones, not stateside bases with high volume public access.

I remained silent until at last I had my turn. "The area of the Presidio coming under protest has maximum public exposure. Things may get problematic." I explained that if the protest got out of hand, SFPD and the California Highway Patrol would be on scene immediately to ensure open passage to the Golden Gate Bridge. That posed issues of interagency planning, coordination, and leadership prior to and in the midst of a chaotic gathering. The protesters were American citizens exercising their right of free expression on American soil. Granted, it was actually US Army soil, and the army certainly secures and controls its own turf. However, it would be wise to consider our geography, media exposure, and peaceful options.

Hawkins looked uncomfortable, and his staff squirmed, looked down, and moved pens around their tabletops. I continued, "We have quite good relations and contact with protest groups. If we reach out to them beforehand, we could save ourselves a lot of trouble."

The room became very quiet. Finally, Hawkins spoke up, "Where are you going with this?"

"Envision allowing protesters to express themselves around the facility on army ground, under strictly spelled-out and mutually agreed-to conditions." The last thing the army wants is filmed scenes of combat MPs scuffling and thrusting twenty-four-inch batons at American citizens. I continued, "We parlay with the protest leaders and propose

a strict protest protocol and walking route, with enforcement responsibility, under agreed-to terms falling exclusively on protest supervisors wearing designated arm-bands. The protesters visibly make their
point, and your guys wouldn't be an active or an 'on-scene' presence
during the protest."

Everybody waited on Hawkins. "You think you can do that?" he
asked.

I replied, "I think there's a chance." We got the go-ahead, and our
"parlay" bore fruit. Two seemingly steadfast opposing entities identified mutual interests and agreed on terms. The day arrived, and the
event went off beautifully, without a hitch. No army uniforms were visible. A couple of weeks later, I received a nice letter of commendation
from the major general commanding the Army Medical Corps. Months
later, I heard that the army contingency plan involved a couple of com-
panies of combat MPs from the 7th Light Infantry at Fort Ord stashed
out of sight in some old warehouses nearby. I was especially impressed
with the military's flexibility, insight, and (I daresay) sensitivity.

DeLorean's $5 Million

Anxiety was palpable as I watched successive $10,000 wads of cash fly
through the air in a rapid-fire "bundle count" toward $5 million. A
chant accompanied the flying greenbacks: "ten, twenty, thirty," all the
way to $100,000. The guys then started on the next $100,000, until
$1 million was reached. It took a while, but they hit that number five
times. Pitch and catch. The money's flight path was an arc from a heavy,
steel cart to eventual deposit in one of several black, heavy canvas carry
bags: it was to be used in the "takedown" sting of John DeLorean, cre-
ator of the innovative stainless-steel, gull-wing car that bore his name
and was fitted for time travel in *Back to the Future*.

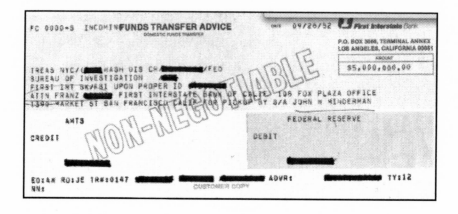

Agent Ben Tisa, who was on my organized crime squad, did a superb job running an elaborate "reverse sting," promising DeLorean cash for drugs. Fifteen black-clad FBI SWAT Agents handled the count at 400 Battery Street and provided escort protection for the cash en route to LA and (we hoped—at least I did) the return trip. George Galloway, security chief for the Federal Reserve Bank and a former Agent, quipped, "John, at the end of this, you're going to know if these guys are really your friends."

The SWAT entourage would fly the money to LA in an FBI plane with an Agent pilot, where undercover Agents would show the money, then DeLorean would produce the drugs. We did, and he did. The hitch—my name and signature were on the Federal Reserve receipt for the $5 million, and I sure didn't have enough lifetime hours left, at my federal pay grade level, to ever pay it back, should it come up "missing." Earlier that day, I'd visited the First Interstate Bank at Fox Plaza and asked the manager to authorize the release of "five mil" of the Bureau's cash. He relentlessly grilled me: "You've gotta be kidding! What's this about?"

I calmly answered, "You know I can't tell you, Franz." Fortunately, the money found its way back in time.

The Rain Hat Bandit

In the early 1980s, my Bank Robbery Squad Agents attempted to identify and catch a robber who typically hit banks Tuesdays through Fridays in the financial district. Regardless of weather, he wore a long raincoat and a signature floppy rain hat. This fashion combo masked his stature and hid, most particularly, the features of his head and face. The robber consistently hovered over the counter, leaned in low, and positioned his torso within the victim's teller window. He then menacingly leveled a four-inch, black, steel revolver directly at the teller's face. He took extreme care to hide the exposed gun and his physical features from view. His confident, commanding presence was extremely threatening. While the robber didn't wear gloves, he was very careful not to leave prints.

His protocol and techniques exhibited disciplined, sophisticated, professional awareness of the need to shield his identity and purpose. Our sleuthing minds said, "Aha…a profile is emerging." His very dark, industrial-type, high-topped leather shoes (exactly the type many patrol cops use on duty) tilted us in the direction that this robber just might be an off-duty cop. We were tentatively exploring that possibility with the helpful SFPD robbery detail when my newest Agent, Kevin Fryslie, a former San Jose police officer, offered to take all the surveillance film and personal descriptive data and work with San Jose PD's sketch artist to create a composite.

Grateful for his insightful initiative, I said, "Go for it, Kevin." He did, and we received, as it turned out, a very good likeness. Since we were a small squad, and SFPD Robbery was tied up, we embraced a long shot by beginning surveillance with just three Agents during the hours when the "Rain Hat Bandit" usually struck. We used Kevin's excellent sketch, and a couple of surveillance photos, and targeted the Rain Hat's hold-up grounds.

On the first day, the Agents parked their car on Sansome Street just before 10:30 a.m. Stunningly, as one Agent was leaning against the car, preparing to get under way, he observed the Rain Hat Bandit, in complete costume, ambling by, northbound.

Agents approached him from the rear, attempting to engage, and the Rain Hat took off running north on Sansome Street, then west down Halleck Alley. Pedaling furiously, a rolling bike messenger sped by the sprinting Agents yelling, "I'll get him!" With a propeller twirling in the wind atop his beanie cap, reminiscent of the 1940s comic-book characters Archie and Jughead, our volunteer pursuer sped ahead then jumped off his bike, the Agents trailing close behind, and tackled the robber on California Street. On the Rain Hat's body, we found the six-shooter used in the robberies. While not a police officer, our robber was a lobby security guard in a nearby building. He'd wanted to be a cop and was studying criminology at City College, but a severe hearing defect in one ear thwarted his ambitions. We were relieved at this arrest, convinced this robber was a true menace to society.

Go East Young Man

My SAC abruptly notified me in September 1981 that, as Supervisor of the Organized Crime Squad, I was to be the Bureau's representative at a major event dubbed "The First International Conference on Organized Crime," sponsored and hosted by the Japanese government in Tokyo in November.

Across the Pacific I flew to engage in three intensive days learning about the Japanese mafia, the Yakuza. More than sixty representatives from scores of countries attended, and each of us contributed a research paper about organized crime. The Japanese were pleasant, attentive hosts, professionally circumspect and reserved.

Prominently positioned near the front of our first-class hotel was a heavily armored and wire-screened police truck, with a large, pivoting water cannon on top, manned constantly by troopers clad in riot gear. Ample back-up police specialist engagers stood by, ready to go. Control in Japan was seriously addressed.

The Motley Crew

In the mid-1980s, SFPD's riot squad was churning overtime to quell demonstrations. Cops loved the overtime pay, plus they got a chance to hit the streets in heavy gear, complete with helmets and batons. No soft shoes for this kind of policing. It was fast-paced, threatening, highly mobile, push, shove, pull-down-the-facemask and let's do it. TV cameras exercised as much influence as bosses.

A block south of the Federal Building, in a park across from City Hall, was an encampment, which served as a visible reminder of the need for low-cost housing—populated by a disheveled, motley mob, punctuated by druggies and boozers, huddled under an aura of legitimacy labeled "homeless."

For a three-day period, activist, sober-appearing protesters surrounded our nearby building, trying to shut down federal offices. The FBI didn't take "shut-down" well. We stayed open and available. Word filtered down that our SAC and the head of the federal General Services Administration (landlord) spoke with the mayor, who supposedly refused to help, quickly resulting in scores of Agents being "shifted to Oakland"—"being unimpeded and unhindered is critically essential to timely response."

As a cop in the 1960s I'd worked dozens of demonstrations and labor strikes, so this stuff wasn't new to me. In those days, SFPD rallied its biggest, youngest cops, threw us together in patrol wagons, and away we went to deal with taunting yells, thrown objects, curses, and upright middle fingers. A shutdown of the Coca-Cola bottling plant at Mission and South Van Ness tested the proverbial "thin blue line," because that's all that existed. About ten of us formed two lines on either side of a narrow, confined lane, enabling "scab" (nonunion replacement) truckers to exit the plant with their trucks loaded. Dozens of enraged union drivers surged, pushed, threatened, and shoved. We "held the line," just barely, knowing that reinforcements seemed unavailable.

One afternoon we jumped off the patrol wagon in front of the beautiful, historic Palace Hotel, on the New Montgomery Street side. The lobby was filled with demonstrators, seated on the floor in rows, with their arms linked side-to-side and their feet thrust underneath the armpits of those in front of them. Standing in the middle of the immoveable mass was a perplexed uniformed police lieutenant. White-shirted, with a gold bar on each shoulder and that distinctive gold slash above the bill of his hat, he wasn't moving: he was trapped, shut down.

The scene was intolerable. Without a word, about six of us began a determined, careful journey, stepping adroitly over the seated mass, until we reached the trapped lieutenant. We stared downward at those sit-in demonstrators encircling his ankles. Nobody dared entrap us. We grabbed that uniformed victim and pulled him free, tiptoeing forward to freedom together. Fortunately, no violence occurred, as it seemed the demonstrators covertly acknowledged that this scene was off everyone's chart. Were there implicit rules of engagement between opposing groups?

Brass Balls

Every year, just before Christmas, a coveted traditional accolade was bestowed—The Brass Balls Award (since discontinued)—given to the Agent who, in the course of duty during that calendar year, had done the most audacious planned action involving a case for which he had responsibility. Nominees for this award, and the written citations detailing what was done to be eligible, were read during a designated morning, with all clerical and Agent personnel present enjoying an authorized post–J. Edgar Hoover coffee break, complete with doughnuts and cookies.

This particular year, I had the Organized Crime Squad and nominated one of my Agents as a candidate. I'd specifically selected and assigned this Agent to a very significant case. He successfully led an interagency task force, which targeted and arrested a drug kingpin who'd previously thwarted and evaded local efforts. The kingpin was federally convicted and sent away for a long time, his operations severely disrupted. While in prison, he was murdered. His funeral featured a lengthy procession through his former community. The Agent decided to put on a disguise and actually drive the kingpin's federally confiscated classic car...in the funeral procession. Indeed, the Agent successfully pulled off this stunt and was that year's recipient of the coveted Brass Balls Award.

Hugh and Cry

The Bureau's core strength comes from the phenomenally diverse backgrounds, experiences, and education of its Agents. Hugh Galyean was a practicing minister in Maryland, close to Washington, DC, when he accepted the offer of a "ride-along" from one of his parishioners, a local police officer. Hugh was hooked and left full-time ministry, becoming a Maryland State Trooper. Eventually, Hugh found his way into the FBI. He excelled in virtually everything that interested him and possessed a special intensity and effectiveness in teaching firearms and survival tactics to Agents and police officers.

Hugh applied his intelligent, experienced doggedness to illuminating the faint, almost imperceptible trail of a cold-blooded, contract killer from Texas who had been on the run for five years. He locked on to a minor, local arrest of the fugitive's girlfriend by the SFPD. She was fingerprinted and photographed after being apprehended for shoplifting at Woolworth's 5 and 10 cent store—filling the corner of Powell and Market Street, where thousands of tourists wait daily to board the famous Nob Hill to Fisherman's Wharf cable-car ride. This swirling, bubbling mass of human anonymity didn't deter or overwhelm Hugh. As a Maryland State Trooper, Hugh had survived a sneak shooting in a road stop, which left him wounded and momentarily shocked, but committed and able to return fire on the fleeing coward.

In pursuit of the fugitive Texan, he followed thin leads back and forth across the dipping and soaring hilly terrain of northeast San Francisco, a massive, highly populated area dotted by distinguished 1920s apartment houses—bars and hangouts spring out like wildflowers in undulating urban meadows. A fugitive hunter eventually begins "feeling" where his prey probably hangs out. Three weeks of walking, talking, and visual scoping brought Hugh into the heart of the Tenderloin—prime, historic crook country. In one of his targeted, afternoon walks, Hugh spied his man and followed him to one of those classic '20s apartment houses, located at Post and Leavenworth.

Hugh's call at about 3:30 p.m. one afternoon aroused me from dull paperwork. I rallied two other Agents and we met up at Hugh's location, a short twelve blocks from the Federal Building. We decided to wait. Perhaps our "Unlawful Flight to Avoid Prosecution" killer would emerge. When Mr. Contract-murder came sauntering out, his intuitive radar and swiveling head immediately detected our move to grab him, and down the middle of Post Street he sprinted. Agent Clyde Foreman, a superior athlete, sped to the front and took him down from behind. Hugh wasn't far behind, and I lagged. Hugh's tracking and honed experience resulted in the dangerous fugitive being put behind Texas prison bars for life.

Gypsy Queen

The final perch in my FBI career was a hybrid—Supervisor of the Applicants and Fugitives Squad. I'd missed Happy Apps in the WFO, and it finally caught up with me. Fugitives were once a mainstay of headline-producing FBI exploits. People were threatened by desperados, and the FBI chased and caught "the really bad guys." However, in a not-well-thought-out decision, the FBI brain trust apparently decided that catching bad guys was just "basic police work." The FBI voluntarily surrendered the primary responsibility for doing this important, eye-catching work to the US Marshals Service, which probably couldn't believe FBI shortsightedness, and their own good fortune. Marshals quickly, whole-heartedly geared up their fugitive-apprehension machinery, and left the Bureau as confused, occasional participants in a field we'd traditionally dominated.

We still "worked" fugitives, but it had slid to third-tier status by the time I received a phone call from a local attorney who expressed an interesting, unusual concern. A female client in her mid-fifties was recently widowed and left lots of money. Soon after, she was befriended and wooed by a Gypsy man who was part of an apparently large, itinerant, extended "family." The attorney provided several names, background info, descriptive data, and details on a Jeep Cherokee SUV. Could we check this group out? I responded, "Why, sure."

The totality of the circumstances met the "reasonable suspicion" threshold, so I assigned an Agent to conduct a limited, basic, preliminary background inquiry. Bingo! Felony murder warrants had been issued in Florida for this entourage. Their M.O. was to target women like our inquiring attorney's client, romance and marry them, then murder the newlywed, cut off the victim's head, hands, and feet, and dump the torso. I told the attorney the results of our inquiry, and he promised his client would cooperate in crafting and executing an apprehension plan and operation.

We created a plan to lure the entire group to one location, selecting a high-end, exclusive hotel on Sansome Street (one-way northbound) in the financial district. Silk's restaurant, which graced the hotel's mezzanine level and featured a Sunday brunch, would be the site of a one-on-one meeting between the selected victim and her potential betrothed. "Family members" were uninvited to the brunch.

Executing a high-risk takedown of a murderous gang required a street location with minimal public exposure, as violence and gunfire were a risk. With the exception of this hotel, the surrounding street area was virtually deserted on Sundays. When the lothario showed at Silk's, we hoped his gang would be waiting in the Cherokee outside, so we could apprehend the whole lot. We'd take down the "family" in the SUV with a Special Operations Group (SOG), boxing in the Cherokee with three or four of our cars. Covering the occupants with overwhelming firepower, we could induce a nonviolent surrender.

SA Gary Rayburn was a key member of our SOG. He still possessed his prized Browning "Sweet 16" shotgun from his youthful hunting days in Louisiana's bayous. He'd been born and raised in Huey Long territory, and I'd seen Gary blast twenty-five clay pigeons out of the sky without a miss when we trained together for the Bureau's first SWAT teams at Quantico. He'd excelled at handling guns and a lifetime of high-risk take-downs.

The Bureau had one standard in planning: identify and compensate for every contingency. Any escape route would have to be north on Sansome toward California Street, so I designated an Agent to be stationed at the California Street corner, armed with a Remington 870 shotgun. When I sought Gary's input, we identified the California Street post as critical. Gary volunteered to "handle it." He'd be playing "lone safety," only needed on the outside chance that things went awry. It never looked that way in the planning stage. As long as he had his Bureau Remington 870, slide-action, twelve-gauge shotgun, Gary "didn't feel alone."

The fateful Sunday arrived and Mr. Romance was apprehended without a hitch, as his luncheon date turned out to be several FBI Agents. Outside, the gang had found an open parking space opposite the hotel. The Cherokee was parked with the driver's side against the curb, but the woman who stayed behind the wheel also had a contingency plan, leaving the engine running. SOG Agents swooped and boxed in the big SUV. She immediately put the vehicle into reverse, burned rubber, and violently slammed directly into a beautiful new Toyota convertible. The Cherokee's massive rear bumper slid, grinding its way up the shiny red car's sloping hood, thereby providing maneuvering distance. An unusually wide sidewalk beckoned to her left.

Between parking meters, up and over curbs, and onto the sidewalk northbound, the Cherokee accelerated. The gang's momentary escape set the stage, and a hot chase seemed unavoidable—except for that scrambling, lone shotgun ace, Agent Gary Rayburn. He positioned himself right in the middle of that potentially deadly sidewalk, directly in the path of the oncoming Cherokee. Dramatically, the Agent pumped the slide action of his big-bore gun and leveled it at shoulder height.

In classic Quantico-taught stance, with that intimidating, powerful shotgun aiming directly at the windshield of the oncoming behemoth, Gary's action compelled the driver, at the last second, to think twice, and she came to a skidding stop. One courageous bayou hunter, representing that thin blue line, played All-American safety on Team FBI, and made the difference with our would-be Gypsy Queen and her deadly crew, who were taken into custody and were soon en route back to Florida.

Sunday afternoon, Gary was in the office finishing up paper work when a call came in from the owner of the Toyota, hysterically crying about his "baby" brand new car being crushed. Gary advised, "Call Mindermann on Monday, and the Bureau will take care of it." When the convertible owner's attorney called, screaming, I explained we would cover all damages—if he could first please calm down. The FBI always makes it right.

Onwards

That final takedown of the murderous Florida gang highlighted many lessons I'd learned and applied over the course of my thirty year career in law enforcement—collaborate extensively in any planning phrase; align assignments with experience and skill sets; rely on instinct and intuition; trust is invaluable; overconfidence is a killer; firepower counts.

Over the course of writing this book, I reached out to Agents and Officers who I hadn't talked with for decades or more, leading to some fascinating conversations. I am grateful to everyone who participated for their enthusiasm, forthrightness, and contributions. I hope that the stories conveyed a sense of what it's like to be a street cop, FBI Special Agent, and Quantico Instructor. Success means you've helped your community and fellow workers.

My formative experiences as a kid in Ames Alley injected values and views, which stayed with me. The men of the SFPD protected and guided me. The challenges and experiences within my policing career were formidable and illuminating. U.S. Marshall Matt Dillon, in the radio drama *GunSmoke,* said, "It's a chancy job and it makes a man watchful." My chance assignment on the weekend of the Watergate break-in led to an unforgettable experience, bringing me face to face with the highest powers in the land. We had little opportunity to contemplate and generate systematic plans. In the midst of chaos, the fate of the day hinged on the focused actions of courageous people.

the native returns to San Francisco

with actor Efrem Zimbalist Jr. from TV series *The F.B.I.*

15

AFTERWORD

BY WILLIAM UPSON

"Hey, nice car." As I parked my brand-new, red GMC Denali, I saw across the street a tall man waving in my direction. Who was he? I finished adjusting my tie in the mirror, then exited and crossed the street, where we exchanged some pleasantries. I then turned to walk to my destination, a monthly luncheon get-together of retired FBI Agents, where I'd been invited by my friend and business client Bob Schildknecht.

When Bob's son applied to college, I helped him obtain an Eagle Scholarship, which I'd established in the early 1990s and over the past twenty-two years has given away more than $100,000 to students. Bob asked if I'd speak to his group about financial planning opportunities—I was in the process of writing my first book, *Long Term Care—Alternatives and Solutions*, and two years later wrote *Pathways to Financial Freedom* about my experiences advising people on investments to achieve financial independence.

Entering the building, I realized the mysterious man, John Mindermann, was headed to the same place. I held the door for him, and we both walked in. During lunch, Bob and I were joined at our table by John, and we shared some laughs. Two weeks later, John visited my Concord office with his wife Carol and several boxes of intensely organized paperwork, saying he liked me and wanted me to manage their investments. "Why, sure!"

Over the next ten years, our friendship gradually developed until one summer day in 2009 when John and Carol visited me to discuss their finances. Talk soon turned to sharing "cop stories," as both John and I began our careers as police officers—John in the San Francisco PD, and I in Connecticut. I knew John was also in the FBI for many years, but we hadn't discussed it much.

Midconversation, Carol nudged John, saying, "Why don't you tell Bill about the time you shut down the White House?"

The time he did what!? With a bit of prodding, John recounted the incredible story featured in Chapter 1 of this book, as Carol beamed with pride. Absolutely stunned, I said, "John, you need to write a book!" That was just the beginning. The more I learned, the more I was overwhelmed by the incredible experiences and accomplishments of this extraordinary man. It seemed ridiculous that he'd never received any kind of recognition or reward for his work. I thought, "This man should be treated with the respect befitting what he did."

My mission became: make Mindermann's dream come true. In my frequent travels around the world delivering conference speeches—on every plane flight, at every meeting, in random elevators—I searched far and wide for a writing partner, always asking people if they knew a great writer or editor who could collaborate in transforming John's stories into a book that informs, entertains, and changes history.

Carol arranged for John to speak at the Trilogy community in Brentwood, Northern California, and I attended with my client Leon Thompson to see John's debut. The crowd was captivated by his stories and Leon asked if John could visit his community at Sommerset.

In January 2012, eighty-five people braved pelting rain to enjoy John's two-hour performance—filmed by Eisaku Tokuyama and James Hall, *Time* magazine photographer. Everyone signed up to be notified when the book was published and pleaded for his return—John was on a roll.

Over the next two years, I met with several talented writers, but ultimately didn't feel the right natural chemistry. I wanted to help John, yet feared my efforts would be in vain. Then my health took a hit, requiring twenty-four rounds of chemo. Weary and frustrated in a hotel room, I picked up the phone and called John to deliver the bad news. With my health compromised, I regrettably wouldn't be able to continue working with him on his book. John was understanding, although deep down, I could tell it hit hard.

Weeks later in Phoenix, my keynote speech at an IRA conference was well received, but I still felt severely under the weather and down in the dumps. Heading home, I boarded the plane destined for San Francisco and settled into my seat. A couple sat down next to me and we struck up conversation. They asked what I did, and I mentioned I'd written two books. I asked them, "Speaking of books, do you know any good writers?"

My fellow passengers, Dave and Jan Philip, told me about their friend, a San Francisco native who grew up on the Peninsula, went to Berkeley, and lived in New York. I gave them my card and they vowed to put us in touch. The next day their son Kevin Philip contacted me and introduced me to Brian Solon.

The following week I met Brian in New York at the performance of my piano teacher, Justin Levitt, at Carnegie Hall. We met the next day in Bryant Park and called John and Carol for our first official introduction. They discovered John knew the father of Brian's friend Joe—retired SFPD Lt. Homer Hudelson, motorcycle cop and accomplished musician. They hit it off and gears began to turn.

A month into writing the book, Carol and Brian somehow pieced together a bombshell revelation—seven decades prior, in the 1940s, John Mindermann grew up on Ames Alley, near the corner of 22nd and Guerrero in San Francisco's Mission District, directly next door to Brian's family. Patrick Ruane, John's friend and mentor who brought him on ride-alongs to play accordion as opening act, was Brian's great-grandfather. Familial bonds spurred our resolve.

Serendipity became a theme. At a chemo checkup, I shared John's story with my nurse Kerry Sherman. She stopped me in my tracks, informing me she was the daughter of Attorney General Richard Kleindienst, who allegedly ordered Mindermann's "White House shutdown." Astounding. Our connection led to a phone call with her mother, providing new direct firsthand insights into what may have really happened.

Karma stuck again when John expressed a desire to donate a portion of the book's proceeds to a cause consistent with his values. He saw a newspaper article describing early-stage heart attacks disproportionately affecting police—recalling his pioneering work in Police Stress and Personal Problems, a course he developed at Quantico and taught worldwide. He asked me what he could do to help.

I contacted Katherine Conrad of the American Heart Association to see how we might work together on a solution to help officers improve their health. When I began telling Katherine about Mindermann's Watergate book, she too stopped me in my tracks, saying, "My mother was Mark Felt's personal secretary." Full circle.

William Upson

ACKNOWLEDGEMENTS

To Bill Upson—a man of vision, integrity, and unflagging inspiration who's primarily responsible for me undertaking the chronicling of these events.

To my wife Carol Ferré Mindermann—who skillfully managed bicoastal writing efforts between Brian and me—infusing her spirit, multiple talents, energy, and enthusiasm, making everything possible.

To Brian Solon, a creative writer of exceptional ability whose storytelling, narrative structure, pacing, and humor inspired our collaboration.

To the "retired folks" in Contra Costa County who seemed intrigued and entertained by my stories—you provided the lift to get me started.

To the men of the SFPD, who stood in the face of threat and menace, against odds beyond calculation, to bring wisdom, guidance, and help to me, and safety and security to "The City."

To SFPD Captain Les Dolan—motorcycle cop, FBI National Academy graduate, and baseball player. With his friendly, engaging manner, he helped my dad and mentored me on the path to becoming an FBI Special Agent.

To the men and women of the FBI, who do an outstanding job protecting our Republic against threats both foreign and domestic.

To the FBI Headquarters and WFO Agents, who frequented the Cuban Coffee House in Washington, DC—great conversations and laughs abounded among us.

To Special Agent Jimmy O'Connor, who nudged me into thinking about a Quantico assignment.

To the WFO's C-2 "Miscellaneous Crimes Squad"—especially Special Agents "Handsome" Dan Mahan, Paul Magallanes, Chuck Harvey, and John Denton—whose efforts exhibited grace under pressure.

To Special Agent Angelo Lano, who displayed determined, even confrontational courage leading our C-2 Squad, and generously shared his insightful new revelations. With his contagious fervor and resolute, unflinching character, he brilliantly choreographed and orchestrated an ever-evolving game plan, which triumphed in midnight dark moments against powerful, entrenched forces and threats to "The American Way."

To Special Agent Paul Magallanes, whose deft, super-efficient development and handling of significant witnesses yielded key successes at critical junctures in the Watergate investigation.

To Officer Charles J. Anderson, SFPD, Star #424, my patrol partner in the Mission 1 car, whose remarkable policing and interviewing skills made The City a better place.

Charitable organizations will receive a percentage of the profits earned from sales of this book to pursue projects helping eligible individuals in law enforcement, including the American Heart Association, the scholarship funds of the Society of Former Agents of The FBI and FBI National Academy Associates, and the International Police Association.

BIBLIOGRAPHY

pg	author	title	publisher
7	Richard Kleindienst	Justice	Jameson Books 1985
15	Frank Sturgis	Warrior	Tom Doherty Associates 2011
38	Max Holland	Leak	Kansas University Press 2012
44	Claire Bond Potter	War on Crime	Rutgers University Press 1958
45	Thomas Repetto	American Policing	Eniga Books 2012
46	Colonel Thomas J. Foley	Most Wanted	S&S Touchstone 2012
47	Lanny J. Davis	Crisis Tales	Threshold Editions 2013
47	Lehane Fabiani Guttentag	Masters of Disaster	MacMillian Palgrave 2012
49	Max Holland	Leak	Kansas University Press 2012
70-71	Francis P. Cholle	The Intuitive Compass	Jossey-Bass Wiley 2011
71	Peter Caddick-Adams	Monty & Rommel	Overlook Press 2012
91	Francis P. Cholle	The Intuitive Compass	Jossey-Bass Wiley 2011
94	Stuart Albert	When: The Art of Perfect Timing	Jossey-Bass Wiley 2013
112	Bratton and Tumin	Collaborate or Perish	Random House Crown 2012
115	Francis P. Cholle	The Intuitive Compass	Jossey-Bass Wiley 2011
121	Steven Pinker	Better Angels of Our Nature	Penguin Viking 2011

129	Streep & Bernstein	Mastering the Art of Quitting	Da Capo Lifelong 2013
130	Dr. Shane J. Lopez	Making Hope Happen	Atria 2013
154	Joseph Schott	No Left Turns	Random House Ballentine 1975
178-179	Mindermann & Teton	Police Personal Problems	The FBI Journal 1977
183-186	Kevin Dutton	Wisdom of Psychopaths	FS&G Scientific American 2012
184	Edward Singerland	Trying Not to Try	UBC Crown 2014
185	D. Theodore George	Untangling the Mind	HarperCollins 2013
185	Hare & Babiak	Snakes in Suits	HarperBusiness 2007
186	Dr. James Fallon	The Psychopath Inside	Penguin Group 2013
189	Michael D. Matthews	Head Strong	Oxford University Press 2014
213	William Upson	Long Term Care	St. Bernie's Press 2000
213	William Upson	Pathways to Financial Freedom	St. Bernie's Press 2003

AUTHORS

John Mindermann's thirty-year career as a police officer and FBI Special Agent pitted him against a crime panorama—thieves, violent street thugs, murderous predators, and a US president. As a street cop with the SFPD, he patrolled San Francisco's roughest beats. In the FBI, he was a firearms and defensive tactics instructor, and leader of the first Washington, DC, FBI SWAT Team. At Quantico, he pioneered innovative approaches for police stress management, crisis intervention, and suppression of violence. He has a BS from San Francisco State University and an MS from American University.

Brian Solon is a writer and editor whose works include *Think Big Act Small, Ignited, Love At First Cut, Illegal Beings,* and *The Road To Reality.* He grew up in Northern California, studied music at UC Berkeley, and produced the global launch of *Star Trek* with director JJ Abrams and Paramount Pictures. He has a JD from Santa Clara University, an MBA from Haas Business School, and lives in New York.